# SIGNATURE WEDDINGS

# MICHELLE RAGO

## WITH FRANCES SCHULTZ
## PHOTOGRAPHS BY DASHA WRIGHT

# *Signature Weddings*

## CREATING A DAY UNIQUELY YOUR OWN

GOTHAM
BOOKS

GOTHAM BOOKS
Published by Penguin Group (USA) Inc.
375 Hudson Street, New York, New York 10014, U.S.A.
Penguin Group (Canada), 90 Eglinton Avenue East, Suite 700, Toronto, Ontario M4P 2Y3, Canada
(a division of Pearson Penguin Canada Inc.); Penguin Books Ltd, 80 Strand, London WC2R 0RL, England;
Penguin Ireland, 25 St Stephen's Green, Dublin 2, Ireland (a division of Penguin Books Ltd); Penguin Group
(Australia), 250 Camberwell Road, Camberwell, Victoria 3124, Australia (a division of Pearson Australia Group
Pty Ltd); Penguin Books India Pvt Ltd, 11 Community Centre, Panchsheel Park, New Delhi - 110 017, India;
Penguin Group (NZ), cnr Airborne and Rosedale Roads, Albany, Auckland 1310, New Zealand (a division of
Pearson New Zealand Ltd); Penguin Books (South Africa) (Pty) Ltd, 24 Sturdee Avenue, Rosebank,
Johannesburg 2196, South Africa

Penguin Books Ltd, Registered Offices: 80 Strand, London WC2R 0RL, England

Published by Gotham Books, a division of Penguin Group (USA) Inc.

First printing, January 2007
1   3   5   7   9   10   8   6   4   2

Gotham Books and the skyscraper logo are trademarks of Penguin Group (USA) Inc.

LIBRARY OF CONGRESS CATALOGING-IN-PUBLICATION DATA
Rago, Michelle.
Signature weddings : creating a day uniquely your own / by Michelle Rago.
p. cm.
ISBN-13: 978-1-592-40254-0 (hardcover)
1. Handicraft. 2. Wedding decorations. I. Title. II. Title: Weddings.
TT149.R34 2007
395.2′2—dc22
2006024531

Printed in the United States of America
Set in Weiss
Designed by Sabrina Bowers

While the author has made every effort to provide accurate telephone numbers and Internet addresses at the
time of publication, neither the publisher nor the author assumes any responsibility for errors, or for changes
that occur after publication. Further, the publisher does not have any control over and does not assume any
responsibility for author or third-party Web sites or their content.

# Contents

*To my grandfather Alfred Conrad Naeole,*

*who is singing in heaven with joy for one of his girls.*

# A Word from the Author

I love designing weddings because I am able to bring my whole life into it. My heritage, my childhood, my interests, and my passions have all inspired not only what I do but how I do it. My wish for you is to understand how my creative process works so that you might begin to tune into your own as you begin planning your big day. By "listening to" what pleases, excites, delights, and inspires you, you can discover your own elements of design and apply them to create your own beautiful wedding.

But your wedding is just the beginning. Whether you realize it or not, your wedding may be a preview to your years of parties to come. And I use the term "party" loosely—I'm talking about anything from burgers on the patio to a seated dinner for three hundred. Your wedding weekend is the first time you and your beloved entertain together as husband and wife. And though your parents may technically be the hosts of your festivities (and lucky you if they're footing the bill), the atmosphere and tone are invariably reflective of you and your husband. Take this opportunity to make the most of it.

As you and your fiancé tap into your own creative potential and allow your personal design elements to emerge, you will inevitably create a wedding uniquely your own, as seen through your creative vision, inscribed with your personal signature. Then you have not just each other, but your heartfelt memories to have and to hold from that day forward. And if there was ever a day to be all about you, your wedding day is it.

Enjoy, and best wishes.

*Michelle Rago*

# SIGNATURE WEDDINGS

# Introduction

*I* am a hopeless romantic and almost always cry shamelessly when a bride walks down the aisle. Weddings are the coming together of two families and a celebration of life, rich with tradition and symbolism, and imbued with the families' own backgrounds and cultures. All of these are factors and influences I take into account when designing a wedding, as well as listening to and interpreting each couple's individual preferences. My role is also to translate the possibilities of a dream into the realities of a well-planned and well-designed affair.

Designing and planning weddings is in a way creating a road map for a couple's future entertaining. The bride and the families involved are often overwhelmed by the sheer magnitude of the event and the multitude of details—so much so that they lose sight of what is important. What is important is the celebration of two people whose love and commitment to each other have led them to join their lives and, by extension, their families. In most cases a religious ceremony is involved and therefore should be approached with a certain reverence and dignity, at least within the context of the church or synagogue. And I think it is very important for the bride and groom to be able to relax and enjoy their day, and for their friends and families to do the same. Helping them to navigate their big event not only gets them through it but gives them a foundation for going forward, for going beyond the wedding day and into the future of what I hope will be many festive occasions together.

My vocation is a natural extension of my love of cooking and entertaining. I went to cooking school and became the director of special events for a hotel—planning meetings, conferences, and, of course, parties. It was the parties that hooked me. I loved the theater of it, and I was especially gratified by the experience of walking into the room with a client and seeing her reaction to what we had created together. But more than anything I became carried away by the power of flowers and how they could transform a room. Hooked again: I had to become a flower designer. I guess you could say my first design love was flowers, and at that point an entirely new world opened up. Weddings were the natural (and to me, obvious) next step.

As I began in wedding design it was all about gorgeous flowers. Then eventually it became painfully obvious to me that in order to ensure the outcome, I had to control the process and most if not all of the major design pieces. (Alas, I never could get control of the weather, however. . . . ) As a wedding designer, I with my client develop and oversee the creative aspects of the wedding: the theme, the look, and all the details to support the overall creative vision. I will participate in designing, partially or completely, everything from papery to linens, to flowers and bouquets, to food, to lighting, to gifts for the wedding party, to whatever. Once the overall design plan is in my hands, all sorts of possibilities for details present themselves, and I will go as far with them as the bride prefers and the budget allows.

There is nothing more rewarding than sending a hand sketch of a cake to a pastry chef and seeing it exquisitely rendered into a tower of buttercream. Or to see a playful doodle become the motif for a save-the-date card or dinner menu. I get a tremendous charge out of it every time. You will meet throughout this book the talented group of craftsmen, artisans, and vendors I work with to achieve a stunning outcome. But the realities of these designs all have their origins in a kind of fantasy, an idea. Be it a drawing, a dream, or a lark, an idea comes from something that inspires you.

We all have sources of inspiration. Even those who do not consider themselves creative have interests and inclinations that inspire them, and when I say "inspire" I mean it in the truest sense of the word, which at its root means "in spirit." Being inspired simply means feeling motivated, enlivened, enthusiastic, and "in the flow."

So, as I work with brides and their families I encourage them to tap into their own deep wells of inspiration, wells we all have—if only we learn to recognize them. (And we will, we will!) Our sources of inspiration are the essence of who we are. And it is that essence I seek to express and to celebrate in my work and in the writing of this book. In addition to its brass tacks information and practical planning advice, this book is about a design process that is universally accessible and that can be applied not only to the planning and design of your wedding but to any creative endeavor you might undertake. Long after your honeymoon suitcases are unpacked and your thank-you notes are written, I hope you will refer to these pages again and again as you and your husband entertain friends and family, and even as you participate in community or charity work, where creative sparks are always welcomed. What you gain from this book may even inspire you to pursue your own form of creative expression, whether it has to do with entertaining or not. Who knows what artistic "aisle" you might walk down next?

Let's stick to weddings for the present, however, and give you a clear understanding of my own design foundations. It isn't mysterious and it isn't complicated. It isn't even a trade secret. I see every wedding I take on in terms of four major components, which become the cornerstones of my design: The Checklist, The S's, The Colors, and The Elements. I will

elaborate on these in the working portfolio chapter that follows, and each chapter thereafter is organized by these four cornerstones. For now, suffice it to say: The Checklist (with variations, of course) covers the items that must be designed, ordered, and produced for nearly every wedding, from the invitations to the bridal bouquet, to the cake, to the guests' favors. The S's are Setting, Season, and Situation. The Colors refer to the color palette by which all design details are keyed. And finally, The Elements are the actual physical subjects or objects that are the core of the design. As you'll see, "elements" as we refer to them in this context might be anything from acorns to zebras. Anyone for re-creating El Morocco for your reception? I'm game if you are!

My own sources of inspiration are at the heart and soul of what I do. They range from the conceptual to the concrete and from the visual to the experiential, but each source sharpens my powers of observation, renews my creative energies, and generates a host of ideas. My sources are constant, continuing, and seemingly infinite. The engines of my creative process, they are what I am and they are what I bring to my work each day, with every bride, and with every occasion regardless of its size or scope. My sources of inspiration are my joy.

My constant interaction with brides is a perennial fascination for me, so much so that it is the inspiration for this book. Brides come in with bits and pieces of ideas and work very hard to communicate the stirrings of their vision. It is my job to be a good listener and to develop their vision into a day or evening or weekend with a beginning, a middle, and an end. I am awed by how the tiniest object or idea can become the heart of the wedding. For example, a sea horse became a recurring motif for a gorgeous wedding in Canouan Island. Sea horses are inherently endearing for some reason, and as creatures of the sea they were totally right for our island theme. Sea horses also mate for life, so what could have been more romantic? The bride had chosen a pair of sea horses to emboss on her invitation, and we integrated the sea horse design throughout the wedding details. We had sea horses hand-painted on the seating cards and menus, but the most remarkable use was having the sea horses embroidered onto the aisle runner for the church. The couple loved it so

much they had the runner made into a duvet cover for their bed. And, of course, every delectable detail like that I file away for future reference and possible creative recycling.

Which brings me to my own personal "creative library," a work in perpetual progress. I keep loads of files, hundreds of photos, and reams of clippings that embody creative elements and ideas. I have two huge corkboards in my design studio. One is my personal inspiration board, which has everything from color chips to fabric swatches to magazine tear sheets. The other is for my bride and acts as a storyboard for the wedding and events surrounding it. As a visual and eclectic muse, a board might include photographs of the reception site, fashion photos, crystals, beads, feathers, fabric swatches, stationery samples, you name it. It becomes a very powerful tool as the event comes together visually. I see it, and more importantly the client sees it. If an element does not work in one place or context, it might in another. It brings to life the editing process, which is as important as the creative production. What you do not do is as important as what you do.

I also spend hours searching for sources on the Internet. I swear you can find everything imaginable online, and it is one of the ways I build a story or expand on a direction. For example, if a bride envisions an equestrian influence for her wedding festivities, I go online and input a combination of words that represent subjects to do with horses and horseback riding. For instance, I'll type "horses, blacksmith, horseshoe" and see what pops up. What it amounts to is a virtual scavenger hunt (my absolute favorite activity as a child), and it often takes me in a direction I never imagined.

## What Inspires Me

Perhaps you enjoy or are inspired by some of the same things I am, and perhaps you will begin to see, as I do, how an object or activity that gives you pleasure also connects you to a higher source of creativity. Say, for example, you love sailing (as I do). Let's see . . . sailing: water, boats, sails, ship's wheel, ensign flags, signal flags, block and tackle, spinnakers, knots, marinas, compasses, sailors, sailors' uniforms, tall ships, dinghies, yachts, buoys, charts, seagulls, celestial navigation. As you can see, a little free association goes a long way, and you can do it with *anything*. Enlist your friends; they'll love it. And look at books, magazines, movies, and the Internet for more objects and ideas related to your original object or idea. Before you know it, you've got more theme, décor, food, and fun suggestions than you'll know what to do with.

Inspiration can come from anywhere. The key is being open to it. That said, if I am to identify my evergreen sources of inspiration, then I would have to say they are

*Travel*

*Film*

*Antiquing*

*The Sea*

## Ideas and Inspirations

| TRAVEL | FILM | ANTIQUING | THE SEA | SHELLS | ARCHITECTURE | PAPER | VINTAGE |
|--------|------|-----------|---------|--------|--------------|-------|---------|
| SENSUAL | BARNACLES | FLEA MARKETS | RURAL CULTURES | DETAILS | BUTTONS | TAG SALES | MOSAICS |
| OLD PAINTINGS | BOOKS | WORDS | FORMALITY | HANDWORK | FOOD | COLOR | SIMPLICITY |

# *Inspiration Board*

## WHY NOT MAKE THE INEXPENSIVE EFFORT TO PURCHASE A BULLETIN BOARD

*and begin keeping track of your own inspirations? It does not have to be esoteric or even particularly artistic. You were impressed by a magazine ad, touched by a note from a friend (on amazing engraved stationery), beguiled by a gallery opening invitation, thrilled by a gift wrapping, charmed by a vintage postcard, struck by a quotation . . . such as Ralph Waldo Emerson's "Life consists in what a man is thinking of all day." You see where I am headed. If it makes you laugh, smile, sigh, or swoon, that object or thought is "speaking" to you. Listen. These are the things that become your own personal storyboard, and you can have it tell whatever story your heart desires.*

## TRAVEL

I love to travel. I have an extensive travel file and take tons of pictures. Half of my photos from trips are of wonderful window displays and close-ups of objects I don't want to forget, like the way the Hotel Savoy in Florence pots the olive trees flanking the entrance, or the way a florist in Capri wraps his flower arrangements. I photograph shop signs and specialty market displays. Perhaps I will borrow from a Parisian cheese shop for a casual buffet layout, with pretty writing on little tin markers to identify what each dish is. Or for a dance I might arrange banquettes and small round tables with vintage black-and-white photos on the walls like they have at Annabel's in London. Or for an outdoor luncheon I might re-create the look of an elegant picnic lunch on an African safari.

My mother's nickname for me is "Wanderlust." At fifteen, I persuaded her to let me go to Greece on a work-study program, which proved to be one of the most transformational experiences of my life. There, in a small rural village on a Greek island, we not only studied Greek culture, we *lived* it. For four months, completely immersed, we studied anthropology, archaeology, Greek history, and literature. I'll never forget our class one day meeting amid the ruins of an ancient mountaintop temple, reading and reciting the poet Cavafy aloud. Outside the class, the work we did had been the work of the people there for centuries: We served in internships at boatyards, sponge factories, and bakeries. That experience sparked a lifelong passion and shaped the manner in which I go about life and my career. Always when I travel I take the time to experience the culture as thoroughly as I can. Other powerfully affecting journeys for me were to South Africa, which I could barely bring myself to leave and, of course, to my homelands of Italy and Hawaii.

## ANTIQUING

Antiquing and flea markets are simply a way of life because I am always on the lookout for unusual and interesting objects I might bring into my work. We recently found great metal fittings from a set of barn doors that we converted for hanging the seating cards for a dinner. I grew up near Bucks County, Pennsylvania, which, with its centuries-old houses nestled among rolling farmlands and charming hamlets, is known for its antiques shops and flea markets. Antiquing is a favorite pastime there. When I lived at home we eagerly awaited *The Princeton Packet* and *Town Topics* so we could scour the pages for the weekend's garage sales. There is so much fantastic stuff to be found at the tag sales and shops in Lambertville, Princeton, and New Hope. People would lie in wait at dawn, coffee in hand, to have first crack at whatever treasures they were sure were awaiting them. Now I spend my weekends in New York City (when I'm not doing a wedding), meandering through outdoor flea markets and the downtown antiques stores.

An array of antique apothecary jars gave me the idea of using similar containers for arrangements for a bride who is a physician. A pair of old, salvaged barn doors became the seating card display for an equine-oriented couple. A shop specializing in all things antique nautical has a beautiful collection of vintage "pond yachts," which inspired the centerpieces for a seafaring groom's rehearsal dinner. Even auction catalogs of valuable antiques or antiquities are potential sources of inspiration, though most of their contents are out of most people's budgets. I recently unearthed the catalog for the late eccentric designer Tony Duquette and his outrageous shell-encrusted furniture. Maybe that's where we got the idea for the "shell chandeliers" we fashioned to mark the entrance to an island reception.

The thing is, I am always shopping for ideas, always looking. I see things that might be used as they are, but just as often I see things that, with a twist here or a change there, might be used as something else.

## FILM

I keep a list of my favorite films and am constantly updating it. I love period pieces and films about society where entertaining is featured. Film to me is a living and breathing visual library and a feast for the senses. For two hours I am engulfed by a deliberately and profoundly stylized world. I will watch a film many times until I eventually deconstruct it—from the clothing to the accessory styling, to the set design. I am probably the only one in the theater who gasped when the ribbon rack was lowered in *Pride and Prejudice.* Because weddings are, in their way, a certain kind of theater, movies are excellent sources of design ideas. I keep a notepad near my film library for reminders and continuing inspiration.

In the movie *Vatel,* for example, Gérard Depardieu's character is charged with preparing a grand feast for visiting royalty. The way he organizes and presents his plans is phenomenal, with sketches, storyboards, maquettes of moving scenery and stage sets, and mock-ups of table settings. He brings the thrill and drama of it to life for his "client," and I love following his lead. As for specific ideas, also in *Vatel,* I've definitely taken cues from the movie's walkways and arbors leading to the outdoor banquet. I've also been inspired by the movie's wonderful scene where an elaborate design of votive candles is created on an expanse of lawn intended to be viewed from above. This, by the way, is a very budget-friendly but visually beautiful effect.

Sometimes the inspiration is more about ambience. *Out of Africa* is just one big styling moment. For its chic simplicity and warm, sensual atmosphere, that film remains for me a kind of visual reminder that less can be lusciously more.

And yet other films, such as *Gosford Park* and *The Age of Innocence,* evoke an era when manners and the maintaining of certain formal social customs not only matter but are a way of life. And while some of that seems irrelevant in today's "casual Friday" culture, I think it is important to retain—to embrace, even—that loveliness of attention to tradition and to detail. Doesn't it make you want to sharpen yourself up a little when you see that?

# Michelle's Movie Favorites

| | | | | |
|---|---|---|---|---|
| Adaptation | 2002 | | Life as a House | 2001 |
| Affliction | 1997 | | Lolita | 1997 |
| Auntie Mame | 1958 | | The Lover | 1992 |
| Baby Boom | 1987 | | Midnight in the Garden of Good and Evil | 1997 |
| Breaking the Waves | 1996 | | The Motorcycle Diaries | 2004 |
| Cat on a Hot Tin Roof | 1958 | | Moulin Rouge! | 2001 |
| Chaplin | 1992 | | Nowhere in Africa | 2001 |
| Chinatown | 1974 | | O Brother, Where Art Thou? | 2000 |
| Chitty Chitty Bang Bang | 1968 | | Quills | 2000 |
| The Cider House Rules | 1999 | | Quiz Show | 1994 |
| Cookie's Fortune | 1999 | | Rabbit-Proof Fence | 2002 |
| The Cooler | 2003 | | Raise the Red Lantern | 1991 |
| Dangerous Beauty | 1998 | | A River Runs Through It | 1992 |
| Dead Calm | 1989 | | Sabrina | 1954 |
| Dolores Claiborne | 1995 | | The Secret of Roan Inish | 1994 |
| Enchanted April | 1992 | | The Shawshank Redemption | 1994 |
| Fargo | 1996 | | Splendor in the Grass | 1961 |
| Finian's Rainbow | 1968 | | Stepmom | 1998 |
| Fried Green Tomatoes | 1991 | | Summer Lovers | 1982 |
| Guess Who's Coming to Dinner | 1967 | | Tea with Mussolini | 1999 |
| Holy Smoke | 1999 | | Unfaithful | 2002 |
| The Ice Storm | 1997 | | Vatel | 2000 |
| Il Postino | 1994 | | Waking Ned Devine | 1998 |
| I.Q. | 1994 | | When a Man Loves a Woman | 1994 |
| Jeremiah Johnson | 1972 | | Wonder Boys | 2000 |
| King Rat | 1965 | | | |

## THE SEA

The sea is where I discovered who I am. It is part of my soul. It is where my heart is. I grew up spending summers at the Jersey shore and have probably traveled to more beaches than to any other vacation destination. I am an avid sailor and shell collector, so many sources of my inspiration come from the sea. I am obsessed with sea urchins and giant barnacles (currently the centerpiece on my dining table). Aqua, blue, and green are my favorite colors! Shells and objects of the sea are a constant thread in my design and clothing. I also use the intricate knots I learned in sailing as fastenings for boutonnieres and bride's bouquets. I once designed a cake that looked like a mosaic of sea glass, and coiled the tops of round dinner tables with beige nylon line (sailors don't say "rope," but

that is what it was). I use grommets repeatedly in papery designs.

Obviously—and fortunately—the sea is a common theme for the destination weddings I work on. And while I emphasize certain aspects that might be specific or pronounced for a specific location—i.e., pink sand for Harbour Island, palm trees for Palm Beach, fishing boats for Portofino (hmm, there's a thought)—I never tire of the sea as a ceaseless creative source.

To summarize, a source of inspiration can be as general and ambiguous as "antiquing" or as sweeping and majestic as "the sea." There are no rules about what inspires you. If you can see it, touch it, taste it, ride on it, or dance to it, there are ideas within just waiting to get out. Some way, somehow, just about any idea can be translated or transformed into a tangible element, and those elements become the basis of my (and your) designs.

# Get Over It!

## OBSTACLES YOU MAY ENCOUNTER IN PLANNING YOUR WEDDING— AND HOW TO DEAL WITH THEM

**BEFORE WE GET INTO CREATING YOUR VISION, I MUST WARN YOU ABOUT**

the possible forces against you, but they are against you only if you allow them to be. These are blockers of the creative process and I want to get them out of the way and out of your head.

### BUDGET

Budget is an issue for many, if not most. But there are many ways to enrich a wedding that do not have to do with being rich. As I mentioned earlier, oftentimes the smallest details have the largest impact, and there are a lot of ways to personalize the details without spending a lot of money. Many things can be written, printed, handmade, or even baked, and relayed through your choice of design. Remember, you are spending money anyway on invitations and a great many other items and details, and it may not cost any more to personalize or customize them somehow. Why not have them reflect your point of view?

We once had a groom who was particularly glib, so we took his clever turns of phrase, added to them, and wove humorous sayings and pithy wordplay into a subtheme of the wedding weekend. He penned the signage—FRIENDS DON'T LET FRIENDS PADDLE DRUNK—by the lake where guests could go out in canoes, and he chose funny quotes to print on the dinner menu in the space between courses. The couple had cocktail napkins printed with quotes from their families that had become endearing inside jokes during the wedding planning process and

were great conversational ice-breakers at the party. One of my favorites was from the Episcopalian mother-in-law-to-be of a Jewish bride who declared, "I'm not goin' up in that chair!" (P.S. Guess who went up in the chair....)

Candy and sweets are another cost-effective source of "customization" for couples. We have had the family dog reproduced as a cookie, filled crystal bowls with the groom's favorite candies, and incorporated cupcakes as a design element because they were the bride's favorite.

Another time I hired a caricature artist to do a funny sketch of the bride and groom that conveyed their personalities and interests. Then we printed the sketch on vellum and spray-mounted it to the outside of cylindrical glass candle holders and placed them on the bars and tables of a cocktail party. It was a hoot—and for only a couple hundred bucks.

The point is, there are lots of ways to add a bit of fun and a lot of flair without breaking the bank. And notice, too, that quite often the best ideas are the simplest and right in front of your nose.

### CREATIVE DIFFERENCES WITH PARENTS

Often the vision of the bride and that of her parents or her future in-laws can be very different. One piece of advice I will give is: "Choose your battles!" Say, for instance, you are a total flower child and your parents are super-traditional. Acquiesce

on the formal wedding invitation and hippie-fy the save-the-date cards, seating card table, and dinner menus. This is where people like me are very helpful. Through patience and a good relationship between designer and family, wonders are achieved. We had one couple, whom you will read about later, who loved the outdoors, wanted a casual outdoor ceremony, and furthermore wanted it in Vermont—all a far cry from the formal Long Island affair the bride's parents envisioned. Well, we found a way to do both, sort of. The rehearsal dinner was kept casual and staged outside around a lake. It was very laid-back but, at the same time, very "done." The ceremony and cocktails following were also held outside at The Equinox resort in Manchester, Vermont, and a seated dinner was held inside, in the hotel's formal dining room. Everyone was happy.

## THE ATTITUDE THAT IT HAS ALL BEEN DONE BEFORE . . .

When I went to cooking school, lest any of us aspiring culinary geniuses labor under delusions of originality, the master chef walked in and said, "It's all been done before. It is up to you to put your personal imprint on your creations." A watercolor your fiancé did on a trip you made together might become the basis of a save-the-date card. A dessert table might be styled as a replica of your grandparents' sweets shop. These are the elements people remember.

# Creating Your Vision

When I meet with a bride or a couple I immediately go about immersing myself in the "culture" of the couple, of course, ultimately to arrive at the culture of the wedding itself. By asking them a very specific set of questions, I seek first to determine what the couple wants to achieve overall at their wedding. Small and intimate, or big and boisterous? White tie and tails, or blazers and khakis? Champagne and caviar, or Southern fried chicken? And secondly, I interview them to identify the sources of the couple's inspiration. And from those sources we derive The Elements of our wedding's design.

## WHAT ARE YOUR WEDDING GOALS?

The following questions are designed to help you define your vision for the look, the feel, and the tone of your wedding, taking into consideration the practical issues of budget, location, and timing. I always encourage my couples to express everything they imagine and to think about the practicality later. There are always creative solutions, and for the rest, there is compromise. What better introduction to married life is there?

Keep in mind that the creative process does not always happen in a strict, linear fashion, nor are the answers to these questions necessarily cut and dried. You may find they are shaded with subtleties or may even change altogether once you've identified your Inspirations and Elements. So go with the flow in the beginning, and stay open to new possibilities. Now, at the risk of seeming to contradict myself, while it is important especially at first to consider any and all options, at some point you have to make a decision and go with it.

You are getting married, remember; you have made that all-important choice. To get there you are going to have to make a lot more choices, starting now. It is true in life as well as in design: You can't kiss all the boys. Trust your instincts and, when in doubt, trust the pros. Don't second-guess yourself too much. And DON'T BE AFRAID OF YOUR OWN POINT OF VIEW. This magical thing we call the creative process revolves around some very realistic practical considerations. Among the areas of discussion will be

*Season*

*Location*

*Bridal Party*

*Ambience*

*Ceremony*

*Music*

*Rehearsal Dinner*

*Food and Drink*

*Papery*

*Color Scheme*

*Apparel*

*Budget and Who Pays for What*

So consider the above issues as you formulate your answers to the following:

What kind of atmosphere are you trying to achieve?

Will the ceremony be during the day or at night?

Formal or casual?

Indoors or outdoors?

Do you want a party atmosphere with a raucous rock band? Or do you see a more traditional affair, perhaps having a big band–type orchestra at the beginning of the evening and a happening DJ later on?

Is the reception going to offer a buffet and passed hors d'oeuvres, or will there be a seated luncheon or dinner?

What kind of wedding party do you envision? If you are a first-time bride, you may have many bridesmaids. If you are a second-time bride, you may have your daughter, your niece, and your fiancé's Labrador. But think about that last one—you don't want to be upstaged by a dog.

How do you see the wedding weekend progressing? Is it just about the ceremony and the reception, or…

Will there be parties and events throughout the weekend?

How will out-of-town guests be entertained? Maybe friends of your parents will host a dinner for out-of-town guests not invited to the rehearsal dinner. Maybe a group of friends will get together to host a dance after the rehearsal dinner that everyone is invited to. For my best friend's wedding in Maine, the couple enlisted all their neighbors with sailboats and had an afternoon of sailing and lunch for their guests. For a New York City wedding, I organized a softball game in Central Park so that the families could get to know one another.

*Design Director, Kim Hirst, buying flowers in the New York wholesale flower market.*

As some of these answers begin to take shape in your mind's eye, I want you to begin delving for your own sources of inspiration—the essence of you, your fiancé, and your families that we will draw from to create The Elements of your unique and wonderful wedding. To begin:

⟶ How did you meet? One New York couple I worked with met in the city trying to hail the same cab. They designed their save-the-date cards with a photo of the two of them in a yellow taxi and a note about how they met.

⟶ Where did you go to school? One couple had the vocal group from their alma mater perform at the cocktail reception.

⟶ How do you like to spend time? As avid game players, one couple put together gifts for the guests comprising wonderful, old-fashioned games like dominoes and Chinese checkers. This was also a nice idea for the kiddies left behind with a babysitter.

⟶ What are your fiancé's and your outstanding characteristics, quirky penchants, or preferences? One groom I especially remember was constantly spouting quotations. So we had them printed on the papery and signage throughout the weekend. We even hung framed quotations on the backs of the powder room doors!

⟶ Is there something one of you adores? One of our brides loves to salsa dance, so the groom took private lessons in secret just to have one salsa dance with his bride at their reception. Now that's romantic.

⟶ What do you do for a living? Two writers, both published authors, wanted words to be an integral part of their wedding design. And they specifically wanted a quote from Dante's *Inferno*. I suggested having a graphic designer take the quote and make a backdrop of graffiti in Old World scripted Italian that we then had silk-screened on fabric. We put a panel of the fabric with the quote behind the chuppah, which is the wedding canopy used in Jewish ceremonies. We used the same fabric for the aisle runner in the synagogue, so they walked down an aisle of words! They loved it!

⟶ And finally, what about your background and your families? One bride's family was from the South, but their very formal ceremony and reception didn't keep them from serving fried chicken and collard greens for dinner, which was delicious! How do you see involving your family? Might your wedding be an opportunity to do something special for someone past or present in your lives? A beloved grandmother's famous cookie recipes were employed as part of one memorable celebration, in homage and memory of her and a lovely personal touch for guests. Comb your attics and photo albums. Dig into your family history. Families can be gold mines of information and inspiration.

*A*s you can see, it is pretty straightforward. Our sources of inspiration are right in front of us all the time. When I work with brides we go through all these questions together, and from different angles. Together we see certain themes emerge, or certain patterns and preferences, and from those we eventually glean the three or four Elements of the wedding's design. These Elements become the touchstones for everything we do, and every aspect of the wedding incorporates one or more of those Elements.

Here are a few quick case studies, which I elaborate on in pages to come:

*The bride loved family summers in Vermont . . . couple enjoys outdoor activities . . . more casual than formal . . . desire to remember a recently deceased beloved grandfather . . . sources of inspiration: involve outdoors, mountains, nature, reflect casual preferences but respect formal occasion . . . We chose as our design Elements: pine tree, birch, acorn, and daisy.*

*Personal Element: boxes of chocolates with bunny drawing on top, recalling grandfather's nickname, "Bunny." Colors: lemon, lime, grass, and chocolate*

*The couple shared a passion for horses . . . both loved candy and had grandparents who owned sweet shops . . . an October wedding was planned . . . sources of inspiration: all things equestrian, an insatiable sweet tooth, the season of autumn . . . we chose as our Elements: horseshoes, candy, orchard fruits, and berries. Personal Element: wedding program printed with photograph of horse they owned together and remarkable story of how they met. Colors: crimson, burgundy, pumpkin, and sienna*

*She adored fashion . . . he was a graphic designer . . . the bride's Danish heritage . . . they loved New York . . . it was a February wedding . . . sources of inspiration: couture and its accoutrements, modernism,*

*dramatic cityscape, nature in winter . . . we chose as our Elements: pussywillow, feathers, and snowflakes, in a dramatic space with the skyline of New York as the backdrop. Personal Element: as design motif, her mother's crown, as worn traditionally by brides in Denmark. Colors: glacier blue, sky blue, midnight black, burnt orange*

Far from limiting, the chosen Elements embolden and empower our creative process by giving us the platform on which to build. As you will see in the chapters that follow, putting that process to work is a dynamic, exciting, fun, and ultimately beautiful outcome.

# A Working Portfolio: Trees and Ferns

veryone has his or her own way of working and of finding solutions and achieving results. My goal in this section is to show you my way—not necessarily so you will copy it (although be my guest!)—so that you can see my process. I believe we can deconstruct or at least demystify the mechanics of the design process as it pertains to weddings, so that whether you are "creative" or not, you can determine your own individual Elements of design and apply them to all the components of your wedding's grand checklist.

# The Four Cornerstones
# of Wedding Design

As I mentioned in the Introduction, I build every wedding design on a solid and easily discernible foundation supported by what I see as my four cornerstones of design. The achievement of any goal is always best accomplished in increments, and weddings are no exception. These cornerstones are:

I. THE CHECKLIST

II. THE THREE S'S

A. SEASON

B. SETTING

C. SITUATION

III. THE ELEMENTS

IV. THE COLORS

There is nothing to do with a wedding that does not fall under one of these four headings, and that knowledge alone should be enough to encourage you to proceed with confidence. Think of each task as a song. You may not know all verses or even recall the entire melody, but you definitely know some of the notes. Begin there and you'll be humming along in no time.

# 1. THE CHECKLIST

I am the first to say that planning and designing a wedding is a daunting task; I am also the first to say it doesn't have to be. Granted, unless you do it for a living it is not likely to be something you will get a lot of practice at. Chances are, however, that almost every single thing that goes into planning and designing a wedding is in fact something you have done before, perhaps many times, and perhaps very well. You've picked out a beautiful dress, ordered stationery, planned a party, arranged flowers, chosen a menu, set a table, organized a party, made loving and thoughtful gestures toward family and friends. . . . See what I mean? Those are all the components of what I call The Checklist. Included on this list are the events, arrangements, and the items needing to be designed, purchased, or produced for your big day or weekend. The overall Checklist generates all sorts of smaller checklists, of course, and the list varies from wedding to wedding, but there is a certain set of basics that are constant. As you see, I've divided them according to which artisan or vendor you would be dealing with for each category, rather than listed the events or items in chronological order of need or use. This way, when you meet with the stationer, for example, you know everything you need from him or her—not that you must order everything from one source, by any means, but you do want there to be a consistency and continuity in quality and style.

# The Checklist

## Papery

- ◯ Save-the-Date Card
- ◯ Rehearsal Dinner Invitation
- ◯ Wedding Invitation
- ◯ Dinner Menus
- ◯ Wedding Programs
- ◯ Gift Tags
- ◯ Seating Cards
- ◯ Thank-you Notes
- ◯ Guest Sign-in Book Concept

## Flowers

- ◯ Rehearsal Dinner
  - ☐ Atmosphere Flowers
  - ☐ Centerpieces

- ◯ Wedding Ceremony
  - ☐ Atmosphere Flowers
  - ☐ Aisle Treatment

- ◯ Personal Flowers
  - ☐ Bride's Bouquet
  - ☐ Bridesmaids' Bouquets
  - ☐ Boutonnieres
  - ☐ Flower Girls' Buckets/ Bouquets/Cones
  - ☐ Ring Bearers' Boutonnieres/Pillows
  - ☐ Flowers for Parents and Readers

- ◯ Cocktail Reception
  - ☐ Cocktail Arrangements
  - ☐ Guest Sign-in Table
  - ☐ Matches/Coasters/ Sparklers/etc.

## ◯ Reception Flowers/Decor

- ☐ Seating Card Table
- ☐ Centerpieces
- ☐ Candlelight
- ☐ Napkin Treatment
- ☐ Chair Treatment
- ☐ Linens

## Food

- ◯ Opening Cocktail Party
- ◯ Bridesmaids' Luncheon
- ◯ Rehearsal Dinner
- ◯ Wedding Reception
- ◯ Sunday Brunch
- ◯ Cake

## Music

- ◯ Opening Cocktail Party
- ◯ Bridesmaids' Luncheon
- ◯ Rehearsal Dinner
- ◯ Wedding Ceremony
- ◯ Wedding Reception
- ◯ Sunday Brunch

## Gifts

- ◯ Bridesmaids' Gifts
- ◯ Groomsmen's Gifts
- ◯ Thank-you Gifts at Wedding Reception
- ◯ In-room Guests' Gifts

## II. THE THREE S'S

THE THREE S'S are your best friends, and like many best friends, they will tell you what to do. Listen to them; they inform a great deal about your overall design. They contain the seeds of your design Elements, which we're coming to, and they harbor many hints at accessories, details, and finishing touches. They are

SEASON

SETTING

SITUATION

The SEASON refers, of course, to the season of the year and should strongly influence your choices of color, texture, and flow.

But within each season are subtleties and nuances that extend design possibilities and further enhance the personalization of your wedding as it is specific to a particular date. There is a difference in feeling and tone between, say, late fall and midwinter. Though the temperature outside may be the same, the trees are bare, and the days are short, the calendar has a rhythm that is dynamic and assertive. Late fall, for example, is about the end of the harvest, "bringing in the sheaves," gathering up the fruits and berries that will sustain us through the winter. It is the time of Thanksgiving, of bounty, and the beginning of a festive period that emphasizes the warmth and closeness of families and home. Midwinter, on the other hand, is restful and quiet and cool. The earth is in repose, but with the innate, knowing energy of anticipation. There is the hope and expectancy of growth and rebirth. I don't want to get too esoteric here, but the point is that beyond the obvious and often clichéd connotations of winter, spring, summer, and fall, the seasons offer marvelously complex subtexts for design. God is in the details, indeed.

The SETTING is just that, the physical location and facilities where the wedding ceremony and related events will take place. Is it the ballroom at The St. Regis or a barn on a cattle ranch? A high church cathedral ceremony or a small, neighborhood synagogue? The setting for each event, be it a rehearsal dinner, a dance, a ceremony, a cocktail reception, or a seated dinner, provides a frame of reference for many aspects of the event: the number of guests, the degree of formality, and the extent to which decorating is required to achieve the mood and ambience you desire. A beautiful room, in my opinion, should be allowed to "speak" and should not be over-embellished. It is the entertaining equivalent of putting on too much makeup.

The SITUATION refers to the set of circumstances apart from season and setting that frame the context of your design decision making. These circumstances may be as broad as "destination wedding," with all its logistical implications, or as specific as "first wedding for the bride, second wedding for the groom; she is Jewish, he is Methodist." Other aspects of The Situation have to do with the time of day the wedding is scheduled, the number of guests, formal or informal, and so on.

The couple's story and the three S's are what lead to the brainstorming phase I label "Ideas and Inspirations." This is where there are no wrong notions and where anything goes because you don't know where it might lead you. I write down whatever comes to mind about your personal stories and your story as a couple; The Season; The Setting; and The Situation. Stream of consciousness—

*random thoughts,* *bizarre notions,*

obvious choices, *unusual tastes,*

and *unfettered imagination—*

all contribute to what eventually will become …

## III. THE ELEMENTS

The ELEMENTS for me is where the magic is. Everything we've covered to this point leads me here, and here is where I really get excited. The Elements, which often derive at least in part from the three S's, are applied systematically to the Checklist of constant components. The Elements are the core of the overall design and inform every creative decision I make and every inspiration I act upon. Some of those decisions seem almost to make themselves, while others are more involved, but either way, the chosen elements are our ultimate creative resource. Arriving at The Elements signals the end of one process of discovery and the beginning of another.

## IV. THE COLORS

I know, I know, there are so many beautiful COLORS out there, it is tempting to want to use as many as you can! Trust me, the more restrained your palette, the more liberated your design. I usually pick only three or four colors, and I do not stray except to variations in tone and shade. This happens naturally in flowers and plant material, and I often take cues from them.

The Season and The Setting are my strongest guides in choosing color, and the colors I choose must harmonize with both. A summer wedding at the beach must be done in bright summer colors, but with a slightly sun-bleached effect. And if there are yellow curtains in the room where the reception is held, the tablecloths and centerpieces need to coordinate. The good news is that this is never as limiting as you might think.

I made the investment in a complete set of Pantone color chips. I am not suggesting you do the same, but you may want to peruse them for inspiration. On hand at any graphic design firm or print shop, the Pantone colors are samples of the dizzying range of colors used by the graphic design and printing industry to specify dye and ink colors for everything from billboards to magazine mastheads, to food packaging.

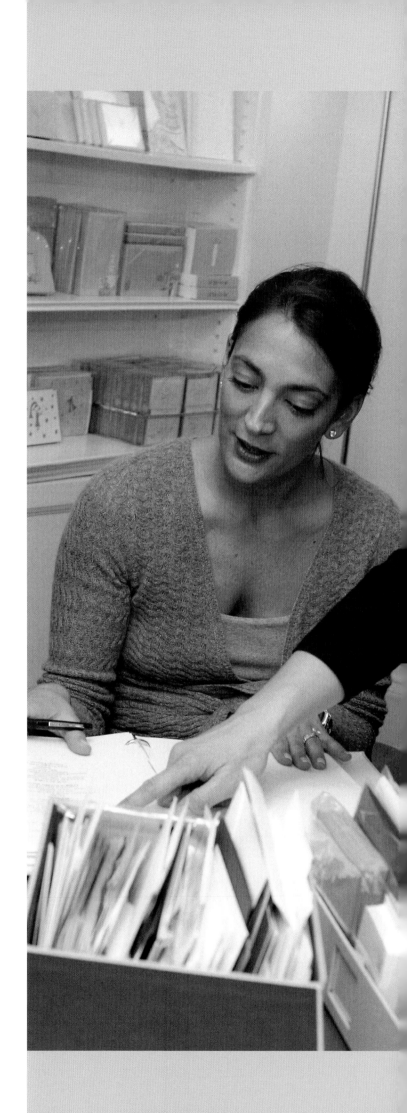

# How I Work

When I first meet a couple I want to know how they came to know each other, what their common interests are, and what excites them about the location they have chosen for their wedding. It is a subtle investigation. I egg them on. I listen. I make notes. Anything goes in the beginning. Then it is a process of refinement—what is practical, what is pretty, what makes them say, "That's it!"

What I seek to come away with eventually, whether from that initial meeting or a series of meetings and research, is the core set of Elements that will ultimately define the overall look and feel of the wedding. Accounting for all aspects of the three S's, a conceptual framework for the design begins to emerge. Just as important are the couple's personal attributes and what each of them brings to the party—figuratively speaking, anyway. A piece of lace from seven generations. A deceased loved one to be remembered. The bride's an artist. The groom's a musician. She loves Twinkies. He loves opera. These personal details inform the rest of the design and become integral points of interest. They are what takes the wedding from being about flowers and food to being about family and beginning a life together. This, after all, is why they come to me in the first place.

The next thing I do is a site inspection where I familiarize myself with the setting and determine the flow of events. What is right may not necessarily be what is most obvious. It is important at this stage to take one's time and to be thoughtful about what it is the couple wants to achieve. A venue or location may have a set or customary pattern for the flow of the wedding's events, but that may not be the best one for you. Cocktails following the ceremony on a beautiful outdoor terrace sounds like a lovely idea . . . unless the sun has already set, and the night turns chilly, and guests still have to make their way to a separate tent for dinner. . . .

Another thing I do at the location is take photos of anything that catches my eye. It might be a stretch of landscape, or a wallpaper pattern, or a furniture arrangement. My initial impressions and these photos are the start of my creative bulletin board, and from there I embark on a free association of ideas that go wherever my imagination and research take me. Broadly, my "mental sketchbook" is divided into the three S's: Setting, Season, and Situation. At some point during the process I give each wedding a title that partially signifies that wedding's Elements of design. Hence we begin with,

## *Trees and Ferns*

For purposes of illustration in this "Working Portfolio" chapter, I chose a setting in my own backyard, the most popular season, and a very typical situation. Getting a handle on the process up to this point puts in place all the necessary groundwork. Our three S's therefore are as follows:

SETTING:

The New York Botanical Garden

SEASON:

Full-on Summer

SITUATION:

An informal, outdoor, early-evening ceremony, with guests meandering among the gardens for cocktails afterward, followed by a seated dinner in the Conservatory.

Hmmm. Okay, that was simple enough. Now . . . let me think. Where can we go with this? What do these three S's make you think of? What about them do you like? What associations do they evoke? What adjectives do they bring to mind?

This is really nothing more than free association, and I keep a running list. I do it out loud, and sometimes for fun the bride and I do it together. I write down all thoughts, no matter how silly. There are no wrong questions here and no wrong answers. Creativity is not about control!

Below are examples of what I come up with:

These Ideas and Inspirations are all influenced by this location and setting. Your ideas will be derived from your particular location and personal history.

## Ideas and Inspirations

| | | | | | | | |
|---|---|---|---|---|---|---|---|
| TREES | | GREEN | | LEAVES | | VINES | |
| | ORCHIDS | | GARDENS | | FLOWERS | | PATHWAYS |
| BARK | | STONES | | MOSS | | BOTANICALS | |
| | WOODS | | GREEN-HOUSES | | CONSERVA-TORIES | | FOUNTAINS |
| FERNS | | SUMMER | | BERRIES | | LIGHT | |
| | LIGHTWEIGHT | | LINEN | | FLOATY | | ORGANDY |
| DECON-STRUCTED | | ORGANIC | | NATURAL | | BRINGING OUTSIDE IN | |
| | NOT TOO COMPOSED | | NATURAL STATE | | PURSES | | FASHION |

25

## TREES

Choosing an emblem is often a great starting point for your own mental sketchbook, as it can be applied in so many ways. For me the tree represents history and strength. Trees are majestic and in this setting compose a natural cathedral where the ceremony takes place. As you will see, the tree becomes the centerpiece of my design, and I completely deconstruct it, finding uses for all its parts and its rich symbolic meaning. For example, a hollowed-out section of trunk becomes a container for the seating-card table, with miniature die-cut trees for the seating cards themselves.

## LEAVES

Almost all trees have leaves, of course, but not all leaves belong to trees, and because leaves are such a versatile design motif, they deserve to be their own Element. In flower design, leaves are basically nature's paper. You can hot glue them, hole punch them, staple them, and curl them. They are beautiful gathered together and striking standing alone. I have used leaves to create cones for the petal toss baskets, die-cut leaves as pages for the dinner menu, and fashioned small handbags of fresh leaves for the bridesmaids' bouquets.

## FERNS

I chose ferns not only because I have a particular obsession with their graceful shade-loving forms but also because they are so easily incorporated into arrangements and other designs. They represent serenity to me and therefore have a calming effect (especially nice amid wedding-planning frenzy . . .). And they have a featherlike delicacy and movement that make them good mixers in bouquets and boutonnieres.

## PODS

When I design I often like to create the juxtaposition between something earthy and something modern. Pods are architectural and spunky and a little bit unexpected. Primal in a sense, sculptural, and constructed, pods lend both substance and strength to a design. A fabulous substitute for something ordinary.

# *The Colors*

MOSS    OAK

FERN    ELECTRIC LIME

*T*aken directly from our SEASON, SETTING, and ELEMENTS, the chosen color palette offers no surprises and calls for no particular cleverness. There is no reason to make this harder than it has to be, right?

Now let's see how our S's and COLORS and ELEMENTS are woven together to produce the beautiful tapestry that is a wedding design.

Let's begin with the invitation. This one is mounted onto a scroll, tied with cotton facing, slid into a stiff, burlap-like sleeve, and mailed in a cardboard tube. The tube is covered with textured paper patterned in a vaguely leaflike ragged effect. The paper, as you will see, is repeated in several other of the wedding details. The invitation is also filled with tiny white paper flower confetti, whose dainty flutter is a small and pretty surprise to the recipient.

*I* feel strongly that the bridal flowers are the ultimate accessory to the bride. Because the New York Botanical Garden is the setting, it seems fitting that the bride's bouquet include a plant considered to be collectible, hence the lady's slipper orchids. And it is always nice to have something slightly fragrant, hence the inimitable sweet pea. Rounding it out are ranunculus and star-of-Bethlehem, which provide buttonlike little punches of color. Moss-green velvet ribbon wraps the stems in a crisscross, leaving them partly exposed. But truly to set this bouquet apart we pulled from the wildness of the gardens and added a fringe of kiwi vine left to sprawl, so the effect is composed and elegant at top, becoming looser and more "wild" at the bottom.

*S*ometimes it pays to think outside the box, and in wedding parlance this might be outside the bouquet as well. Our team created bridesmaids' "purses" made from leaves and "encrusted" with star-of-Bethlehem and hydrangea. We bought cheapie purses and used them as the under-form, sewing on their botanical coverings using a hole punch and grass "thread." It was a little wacky but also playful and fun.

The boutonniere is one of my favorite accessories in this whole design scheme, encompassing all four of our Elements—liberally interpreted—in a charming, compact form. Tiny cones are made from leaves and slipped into a corkscrew-shaped piece of kiwi vine, secured at the bottom with covered wire. Filling it are chartreuse lanuginosa berries, star-of-Bethlehem, and a perky piece of fern.

To create the ceremony space we chose an existing arbor in the garden, marveling at its beautiful placement in a clearing sheltered by tall trees. But we didn't want the trellising to get lost in all that green, so we needed to make it stand out somehow. To accomplish this we wound it with big, sweeping spirals of grapevine to create a graceful, fluid form. Then we wired it with Peegee hydrangeas—so puffy and feminine—and trimmed it with a showy fringe of hanging amaranthus.

31

We made the petal toss cones for this wedding a bit bigger than normal so they wouldn't get lost amid the huge trees and greenery. Being slightly adventurous with size and scale is another way to be out of the box, creatively speaking, and also a little more modern. The cones themselves are made from large leaves, stapled with a regular stapler and secured by covered wire. We covered the staples with ribbon and added ribbon handles anchored by twigs. Instead of the usual rose petals, we filled the cones with Peegee hydrangea petals, which are abundant in this region during summer and therefore very reasonably priced.

ith the ceremony complete and the petals tossed, the bridal couple and guests will linger for cocktails. Normally the favors for guests are placed near the exit for them to take as they depart, but it could be a nice change to present them at cocktails. Particularly if guests have come from far and wide and there are many who do not know one another, this early gift presentation gives them a little something to talk about—maybe that's why they call them favors? This would be particularly true in the case of booklets of family recipes. With a tree on the cover and a reference to the idea of a family tree, the booklets embraced our design Elements and gave them an endearing personal touch. The twig binding is secured with knotty twine, and the booklets were stacked in wooden boxes lined with leaves. For anyone who might miss them at cocktails, the booklets in their box are easily transported to be near the exit by the end of the evening.

# The Seating Card Table

## AS COCKTAILS WIND DOWN AND GUESTS MAKE THEIR WAY TO DINNER,

one of the first things to greet them is the seating card table, so it is very important visually.

Do you remember dioramas and that almost magical feeling they evoked? They fascinated me as a child and they continue to, to this day, so when I got the idea for this hollowed-out tree trunk I thought it would make a perfect little diorama. Laid on its side, the trunk offered several openings for peeking into, which we filled with all sorts of ferns, coleus, mosses, pine needles, and acorns. It was like looking into a glade of some enchanted forest. (Definitely try this at home because you easily could!) The die-cut paper trees are fitted together so they can stand upright, bearing the name of the guest on one side and the name of a tree on the other. The tables were given tree names instead of numbers, which not only reinforces our design elements but also obviates any sense of hierarchy among the tables, lest Aunt Gertrude take offense at the placement. But please, if you have a lot of tables, ten or more I'd say, please arrange for staff to have seating charts to assist your guests in finding their way.

When there are going to be more than six or seven tables, I generally do alternating centerpieces to enhance the visual dynamic of the space and to keep the eye moving. (Besides, in some instances twenty of the same centerpiece can be boring.)

As I was surfing the Internet in search of botanical-related anything, I was thrilled when I came across these miniature Victorian terrariums that echoed the fabulous shape of the botanical garden's famous conservatory. Striving for that deconstructed, organic look, I arranged it open, rather than closed, to look as if the plants were growing out of it—coleus, ferns, eucalyptus, and poppy pods. Bits of moss were added to the terrarium to make it looked aged. The table names, which were trees, were written alongside botanical sketches of the species of tree, mounted to a silk-covered board.

For the second centerpiece, disks of birch trunk were assembled and glued to create the base of free-form arrangements of fern, coleus, eucalyptus pods, lisianthus, phalaenopsis orchids, and scabiosa pods.

# Cake

## TOWARD THE END OF THE EVENING AND TO THE DELIGHT OF ALL, IT IS TIME

to cut the cake—a special and climactic moment when all eyes turn again to the couple—and to the cake itself, of course. The cake is the ultimate wedding accessory. Like seating card tables and papery, the wedding cake can make a grand statement. Photographed for posterity, the cake-cutting is often the shot that ends up in the big silver frame on the piano or in your mother-in-law's living room, with the cake featured as prominently as the bride and groom. All the more reason to create something really "wow."

It is my belief that the cake should be left to the end, after your overall design has really gelled. The cake is the place for you to strengthen your existing design and to reinforce it where needed. As a willing and broad canvas, the cake design might emphasize or repeat one of your striking design Elements, or it might combine several Elements. And as the cake is often spotlit in the center of the room or tent, it becomes the reception's crown jewel.

Consult your inspiration corkboard. If family traditions are a part of your theme, you may want to replicate the cake your parents or grandparents had. Or you may want to depart

from tradition entirely. If you love chocolate and strawberries, go for it. Or have chocolate icing with a layer of white icing on top. The possibilities for structure and design are limited only by your and your baker's imaginations.

In this case we worked with premier New York baker Ron Ben-Israel to come up with an idea that encompassed all of our Elements, and he did not disappoint. Ron's team took a fairly literal approach and borrowed from nature as well as our own nature-inspired completed designs. Leaf cones with hydrangea petals become the dividing pillars between the tiers, and the tiers are festooned with ivy, fern, and all of the flowers in the bouquets.

There are also lovely customs surrounding the cake. Saving and wrapping the top tier to freeze and thaw for dessert on your first anniversary is one. Guests taking cake home with them is another—and another design opportunity to create wonderful little boxes or bags to put individual pieces of cake in. The idea is that if an unmarried lady or gentleman sleeps with a piece of wedding cake under the pillow, they will dream of whom they will marry.

If I had to write a slogan for this wedding, it might be "Love 'em and leaf 'em." The menu cards are made from die-cut oak leaves attached with screw posts, one leaf per course, with the writing in white ink. The white square plates and brown organdy napkins lend a modern feel—sophisticated and somewhat unexpected.

In the chapters that follow you will see real weddings and learn how other couples have discovered their own personal Elements. An inspiration becomes a concept, which becomes an Element, which becomes the core of your design, which you then apply to your components. Each builds on the four cornerstones: The Checklist of wedding components; The three S's; The Colors; and The Elements of design. If you adhere to the principles we've outlined in the Introduction and Working Portfolio, going by the structure we've established, you are sure to find your way. And what a beautiful and exciting journey you will have!

# Acorns and Daisies

*T*he first time I met Gerri and Brett I was immediately struck by their enthusiasm and self-confidence. They just *knew* they could make their wedding a special experience, not just for themselves but for their guests as well. Their sense of fun and creativity and their devotion to each other never waned during the process. Both Brett and Gerri were involved every step of the way, which doesn't always happen—or happen successfully. It was a team effort and the team won!

Gerri's family owns a house in Manchester, Vermont, where she grew up, going season after season. Both she and her fiancé have a love of the outdoors, so for them a fresh-air wedding in Vermont was the answer. At the beginning, the only components they were completely certain about were the location and style of ceremony. The service had to reflect both Gerri's Jewish heritage and Brett's Episcopalian background. They also knew (thank goodness) that a good dose of whimsy and humor should be included throughout. Brett's winning way with words would come in handy here. And last but not least, as the traditional rehearsal dinner (and good old-fashioned roast) would be hosted by the groom's family, this would be the place for a loving but lighthearted nod toward Brett's recently deceased grandfather.

Gerri, Brett, and I spent hours exploring every creative possibility in order to personalize the day to reflect both families' sensibilities. I have no doubt that for Gerri and Brett family holidays will be fun and thoughtful flurries of creativity for years to come.

## Season:

Late Summer

## Setting:

An elegant country inn in Vermont

## Situation:

The bride and groom love all things outdoors and are inclined to a more casual affair. The bride's parents favor a more traditional, country club setting. Need to please both. The bride's family is Jewish; the groom's Episcopalian, and the groom's beloved grandfather is recently deceased.

## Ideas and Inspirations

| | | | | | | | |
|---|---|---|---|---|---|---|---|
| VERMONT | LANDSCAPE | PICTURE POSTCARD | RUSTIC | WOODSY | TEXTURE | BURLAP | SOUVENIRS |
| PINE TREES | PINE BARK | PINE NEEDLES | PINE SCENT | MOUNTAINS | CONES | ROCKS | SHAPES |
| BRANCHES | TWIGS | WATER | LAKE | CANOE | PADDLE | CABIN | BARK |
| SUMMER | CASUAL | BAREFOOT | FLIP-FLOPS | FLOWERS | DAISIES | HYDRANGEAS | BERRIES |
| PETALS | RIBBONS | GINGHAM CHECKS | BROWN | TREILLAGE | BASKETS | GREEN | SKY |

# The Elements

## BIRCH

I am particularly partial to the versatility of birch. Whether paired with something modern or used on its own, birch always takes on the challenge. Birch can be purchased in many forms today: shavings, tiles, and flat panels. There are also beautiful birch papers.

## ACORNS

Green acorns instead of brown keep the season keyed to summer, and they make fantastic finishing details for the personal flowers. Mother Nature has provided us with endless possibilities for bits and flourishes in design.

## SEA GRAPES

Whenever you are working with a lot of green, it is imperative to create texture. Berries like these sea grapes are a wonderful way to achieve texture in any design. What is unique about these berries is their uniform size and nice, glazed finish.

## DAISIES

Daisies. I just don't know if there is a happier flower. Daisies are a wonderful choice if you are interested in using only one type of flower. And because they are bright white and yellow, they "pop" against almost any backdrop.

## PINE TREE

This region of the country is blanketed in pine trees and it seemed obvious to make it an emblem of the wedding and the core of the design. They are striking and majestic and almost impossible to distract from. They also have a beautiful, clean fragrance that permeates the air.

## PINECONES

Pinecones are gorgeous and architectural and work perfectly in a repetitive pattern. Like shells, pinecones are one of nature's works of art and so much fun to design with. There are also many shapes and sizes and they are available twelve months of the year.

# Colors

| | | | |
|---|---|---|---|
| LEMON | | GRASS | ● |
| LIME | ○ | CHOCOLATE | ● |

## The Details

My initial trip to Manchester, Vermont, generated an arsenal of beautiful concepts, not the least of which was the sculptural quality of the pine-covered mountains. Pine trees became the inspiration for all the papery, including the invitations, save-the-date cards, gift tags, menus, and signage.

I think of the papery as a suite, with a unifying element, but it doesn't have to be the same thing over and over again. The magic is in the variation. For destination weddings, I suggest creating a more formal look for the more formal pieces—the invitations, menu cards, and seating cards. Then I have a more whimsical version for save-the-dates, signage, and gift tags. That way the design doesn't get stale, and you avoid the appearance of branding.

The save-the-date card is another area where you can set the tone. Gerri and Brett took a photographer into Central Park in New York City (where they lived) with hand-written signs reading SAVE, THE, and DATE. The photos were developed into a filmstrip format for the cover of the card and a pine tree sketch was incorporated into the wording.

I also believe a strong design concept should have a strong finish. A sweet idea the bride created was to make postcards from a photo of the couple, stamped and addressed to their new home, with a note inviting guests to write the honeymooning couple a card. It is wonderful to have a bunch of fan mail waiting for you when you return home!

$\mathcal{F}$riday night was all about this glorious summer setting and getting to know one another. I believe in always addressing the entrance. It's the first impression of the party and sets the tone for the evening. A sweet boathouse on a tranquil mountain lake was the final stop after crossing this little footbridge draped with greenery and a sprinkling of daisies. Flip-flops, tied together with ribbon bows and piled in a galvanized box, are an invitation from the hosts to kick off your shoes and have a good time.

Gerri and Brett worked with wedding planners Claudia Hanlin and Jennifer Zabinski of The Wedding Library in New York City to infuse the evening with activities and entertainment. A local fiddle player was hired to liven up the place and instill a little local flavor, which is especially nice at a destination wedding. Ancestral roots were acknowledged as well, with father and son dressed in their family's tartan.

# The
# Rehearsal Dinner

**THE REHEARSAL DINNER, TRADITIONALLY HOSTED BY THE GROOM'S FAMILY,**

is sometimes the first event where, after months and months of planning, the host families can relax and really begin to enjoy themselves. The arrangements are made, the work is done or in progress, the guests have arrived, the moment has come. For the guests, the dinner is a great icebreaker, often the first time some are meeting one another, brought together by a happy occasion.

Different regions have different traditions. In the South and Midwest it isn't uncommon to have an emcee for the evening, usually a poised and trusted friend of the groom or the groom's family. He generally signals the first toast to be given and takes it from there, recognizing the next person who would like to give a toast or say a few words. In case of a lull, he steps in to keep the evening and the remarks running smoothly.

Rehearsal dinners are probably the best place for toasts and other sweet moments, scripted or not, if there is no seated dinner after the wedding. It is also the more intimate gathering of the two. Too many toasts and activities during the dinner reception can kill the evening's momentum. The deal is done and all are ready to kick up their heels a bit.

For a destination wedding, the rehearsal dinner can truly set the tone. Anything ranging from a lobster bake on the coast of Maine to a buffet dinner at an auto museum might set the stage for festivities and design delights to come.

The rehearsal dinner given in the hometown is a little different from the rehearsal dinner at a destination wedding. It is a bit tricky if all out-of-town guests are not included,

because after all they have made a considerable effort to get there, and you want to be a gracious host. My thinking is that you are obligated to entertain or at least provide options for all out-of-town guests, but this does not necessarily mean having all to the rehearsal dinner.

One option is to limit the rehearsal dinner to wedding party and family, thereby clearly delineating who makes the cut and so avoiding hurt feelings. Another idea is to have welcoming cocktails for all before the dinner, or a party for all when dinner is finished. In case of the latter, friends of the family or bridal couple may get together and host a dance. Family and friends may also offer to host smaller, informal dinners for out-of-town guests not invited to the rehearsal dinner.

If you are lucky enough that your budget allows you to have the rehearsal dinner be all-inclusive, you need to be careful to distinguish that evening from the one to follow. In other words you don't want the rehearsal dinner to trump the wedding. This would be an opportunity to contrast the events in tone and dress. Aim for a level of intimacy or informality at the rehearsal dinner. Acknowledge family traditions or other important people in your lives. The wedding is about the couple; the rehearsal dinner can be about your friends and families and their importance to you. It doesn't have to be solemn or serious, which the wedding requires to a certain degree. Let your rehearsal dinner be fun and spontaneous!

planned, participatory activity is a wonderful ice-breaker for guests, not to mention good photo fodder. And what's a mountain lake without canoes gliding to and fro? Everyone got into the spirit and paddled away—responsibly, of course. Posted nearby, planted firmly in cheek, was an oar painted with FRIENDS DON'T LET FRIENDS PADDLE DRUNK, courtesy of the mischievous groom. Candlelit lanterns shone on the path to the boathouse where dinner was held. Adirondack chairs on the bank of the lake provided suitable seating for spectators and were a thoughtful consideration of older guests.

As I mentioned in the Elements section, I feel daisies are one of the happiest flowers and one of my personal favorites. I was thrilled that Gerri chose them for the core of her rehearsal dinner design. We took an eight-foot table, draped it in yellow and white gingham, and covered the top with flats of grass. We then water-tubed individual daisies (which, by the way, takes a bit of time) and nestled bright white seating cards with daisy-yellow grosgrain ribbon and little cotton daisy buttons in the grass.

The groom had a wonderful idea of memorializing some of the funny quotes said by family members throughout the planning process on cocktail napkins placed strategically at the bars. Guests had a rousing time trying to sort out who said what!

*F*or the rehearsal dinner we dressed the tables reflecting summer in sunny yellow gingham. Napkins tied with gingham bows bespeak summer informality, freshness, and fun. Oversized daisy balls were suspended from tree branches, and the centerpieces were simply trays of wheat grass "planted" with daisies. Pillar candles wrapped with yellow gingham ribbon set on the tables and grouped on the boathouse steps cast a wonderful glow as the twilight falls.

As is sometimes the case with one or even both of the families involved in the wedding, a loved one may have recently passed away. Honoring that person's memory during a wedding celebration need not be—and should not be—maudlin. Here the groom's grandfather, fondly known as Bunny, was acknowledged in a lighthearted but respectful way as part of the rehearsal dinner, appropriate since the groom's family hosted the evening. Bunny chocolates were tucked in a box with a card courtesy of the couple that read, "In sweet memory of Bunny—his prints are everywhere."

# In Loving Memory

## A WEDDING CAN BE AN EMOTIONAL TINDERBOX. EVERYONE CLOSELY INVOLVED

*is all at once excited, thrilled, nervous, terrified, happy, sad, hypersensitive, hyper-everything. If a loved one has recently passed, the loss is naturally felt very keenly at celebrations of family closeness and love. Acknowledging that person in the course of the wedding festivities is a way of honoring not only his memory but the love and affection felt for him by those who knew him. This is a very personal choice, and how you go about it may range from a special passage in the wedding program, to a few words from the officiant during the ceremony,*

*to a lighthearted sentimental gesture like the one Gerri and Brett made with bunny-shaped chocolates. In another case we styled a candy station with vintage photos of deceased grandparents who coincidentally both owned sweet shops. The point being— remembrances need not and should not be heart wrenching; a wedding is not the place. Honor the memory of loved ones by honoring the joy of their lives and the joy they undoubtedly would wish for you as you begin a new life in marriage.*

$\mathcal{T}$hank goodness the weather held for us on the night of the ceremony. Forgoing the typical flowery design, we used all natural elements such as green acorns, pinecones, and a range of green berries to accentuate the very woodsy but modern design. The wedding canopy, or chuppah as it is called in the traditional Jewish ceremony, is wound with woody grapevines and puffs of white hydrangea.

*B*rett put his verbal skills to work in creating the wedding program incorporating both Jewish and Episcopalian traditions. Presenting the programs in a birch-covered box reflects the care and thought that went into writing them.

# The Petal Toss Box

## IN ANCIENT GREECE, AFTER THE WEDDING FEAST, EVERYONE WALKED WITH

*the bridal couple to their new home. The singing crowd strew the couple's path with flower petals, whose sweet fragrance was released as the couple and crowd trod over them. Petals and grains were also tossed to ensure the couple's happiness and fertility. Today's more modern concept has guests showering the bride and groom as they leave the ceremony rather than as they leave the reception, which nowadays the newlyweds may be the last to do. We love coming up with*

*beautiful petal toss concepts as they are like little jewels adorning the aisle.*

*Keep in mind, however, that every church, reception location, park, and outdoor ceremony area has policies about what they will and will not allow to be scattered about their premises. Take the time to find out and choose your petal toss box filling accordingly. You don't want the head gardener running after you in a fit of anger. We've had it happen—not nice.*

*T*he petal toss box, covered in birch bark fastened with sage satin ribbons and acorn tops, is a juxtaposition of hard and soft textures which gives a sophisticated look to even the simplest design Elements.

toss
to
a
rosy
future

The personal flowers are another opportunity to incorporate your chosen design Elements in a simple manner. It's not about white anymore. Gerri's bouquet is studded with acorns and fastened with the same green satin ribbon and acorn "buttons." Keep in mind when working with acorns that they tend to pop out of their little caps when they are handled a lot. A touch of hot glue will keep them together.

*O*ur precious flower girl, Emma, wears a crown of pinecones and spray roses and carries a birch cone filled with chartreuse sepals of hydrangea and finished with green acorns and baby pinecones. It was tough, though, to convince Miss Emma that she was to hang the cone on her wrist and not around her neck!

*W*here is it written the boutonnieres for men all have to be the same? *They don't all have to be the same!* I love having them slightly different yet all in the same color palette. Forgo the obvious flower for an acorn or pinecone.

And though the look for the reception was decidedly dressy (which pleased the parents), we maintained a rustic outdoorsy feel (which pleased the bride). An excellent example of this was the seating card table design, which I firmly believe should be interesting and well thought-out. If you are having a seated dinner, it is the first thing guests interact with when they arrive at the reception. Here seating cards are securely tucked into a ribbon and pinecone lattice. Instead of the usual big flowery centerpiece we planted woodsy terrariums in tall modern cylinders. Keep in mind that the wind plays a major role during outdoor receptions and seating cards need to be protected from the wind, especially in Vermont.

$\mathcal{D}$raping doorways with vines and flowers is a nice way to soften a façade as well as to announce the entrance. Grapevines, green cymbidiums, pinecones, and roses mark the entry to The Equinox, where guests had cocktails in the garden before going in to dinner.

With birch trees in the background conveniently providing the palette, moss-colored grosgrain greenery is woven into chair backs, and cushions are covered in almond dupioni silk. The tablecloths are cocoa dupioni silk with a cream cuff. They were just as beautiful inside as they were outside where we took the photograph.

Centerpieces echo the terrariums at the escort card table, with plain glass cylinders of varying sizes holding green shadow hydrangeas, cymbidiums, star-of-Bethlehem, lanuginosa, green coxcomb, sea grapes, and Eskimo roses. Candles are floated in taller containers weighted with river stones. The acorn-green hemstitched napkins are dyed to match and topped with a beautiful snippet of green acorns, a rather extravagant detail without extravagant expense. Besides, every well-set table deserves a freshly ironed and starched linen napkin.

A wedding design that incorporates bright colors and cool, crisp fabrics keeps the tone cool and the feeling light. Our Vermont wedding was a perfect example of this. Even in New England, midsummer weddings can be hot, humid, and rainy! As Gerri's parents reminded me throughout our planning, "Michelle, you know the old adage about Vermont weather, don't you? 'Just wait five minutes; it will change!'" But nothing could dampen the spirits of Gerri and Brett's guests, who wished the new couple a life full of sunshine.

# Feathers and Snowflakes

For Heather and Jared a winter wedding in New York was a destination wedding, as exciting and as glamorous as it gets. The downtown Sky Studios, a posh private residence available for special events, offered a stylish and intimate setting as well as heart-stopping views of the city. Garden terraces and a pool enhanced the venue's appeal even more, accommodating perfectly the couple's desire to create, as Heather says, "an evening that feels like a congenial cocktail party at an amazing New York City apartment."

Ohio natives and high school sweethearts, Heather is a medical student and Jared a graphic designer. Both are highly creative and love the energy and edge of the city, which was clearly reflected in their design choices. By the time they came to me, Jared had already designed their save-the-date cards and wedding invitations, giving us a ready-made color palette of aqua, orange, and black with touches of cream. Heather, who loves fashion and has a theatrical flair, wanted anything wintry and everything textural—branches, crystals, fur, feathers, and snowflakes.

And while this couple's outside-the-box thinking (which I loved) gave the wedding a nontraditional aspect, we did want to acknowledge traditional sentiments. Heather's family and Swedish heritage were very important to her, so we included them with certain decorative elements. For example, in Swedish culture, brides of noble descent are meant to wear the family crown during the ceremony. This one was Heather's mother's from the 1950s, which we displayed in a place of honor. And as a parting gift, guests received a small package containing Heather's grandfather's old family recipe for glogg and a packet of spices needed to make it. Glogg is a hot and potent libation that helps to lighten those dark Swedish winters—and warm the chilly New York nights.

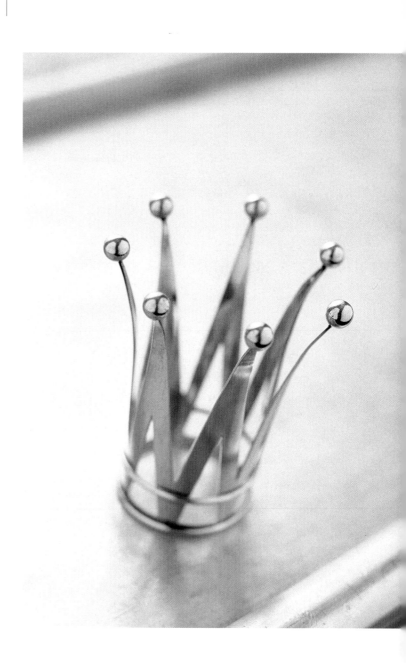

## Season:

Midwinter

## Setting:

Sky Studios in downtown New York. A triplex penthouse loft with multitiered outdoor patios, a pool, and panoramic views of the city.

## Situation:

A sophisticated and fashion-forward bride for whom marrying in New York is considered a "destination wedding." Evening ceremony and reception to be held in one location, with guests needing to shift from one room to the next. Cocktails and passed hors d'oeuvres preceded a buffet dinner with a dessert bar. Late-night dancing.

## Ideas and Inspirations

| | WINTER | | SNOW | | CRYSTALS | | SNOWFLAKES |
|---|---|---|---|---|---|---|---|
| ICE | | ICE FAIRY | | FASHION | | COUTURE | |
| | COUTURE DETAILS | | FEATHERS | | BLUE | | EARTHY |
| TEXTURE | | BRANCHY | | STRIKING | | WARM | |

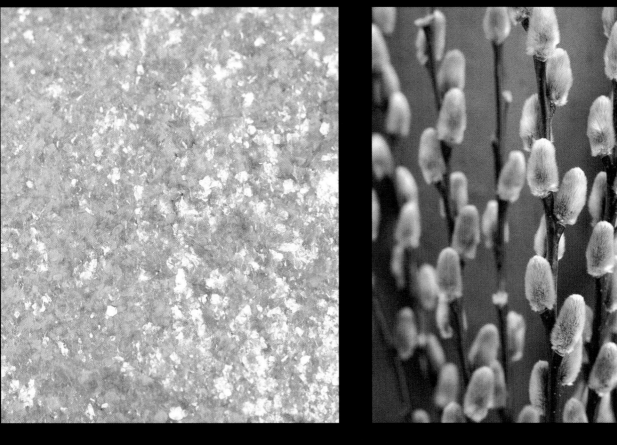

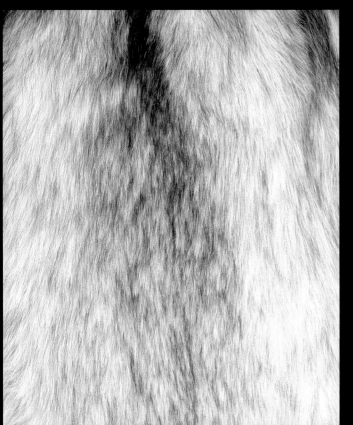

## SNOWFLAKES

Snowflakes are the ultimate of nature's astounding artistry. We prayed for the real thing during this winter weekend in the city, but Mother Nature did not oblige us. So instead we made our own from sparkling mica flakes, which were fortuitously weather-oblivious.

## PUSSY WILLOW

Pussy willow is one of the most beautiful winter branches and its buds are like fur. They are also flexible, which makes them easy to manipulate in lots of different ways. We even used them in the boutonnieres.

## FUR

My first meeting with Heather was spent reviewing photos of all of her fashion picks and the different ensembles she had put together to wear the night of her wedding. She changed several times throughout the course of the evening, and fur seemed the perfect Element to accent the design. The pussy willow is nature's perfect execution of furry texture.

## FEATHERS

Feathers have a soft, tactile quality and at the same time a certain coolness. They're also flirty, feminine, and seasonless.

# Colors

GLACIER BLUE    MIDNIGHT BLACK

SKY BLUE    BURNT ORANGE

# The Details

The groom is a graphic designer and applied his considerable skills to the papery design. The save-the-date card was a particularly interesting use of color, with aqua type on a black background. The invitation was the more conventional black type on cream paper, but with a bold black-and-white stripe that showed through from the back.

Our setting was a bit unusual for a wedding in some parts of the world, but not for a wedding in New York City. Sky Studios is a triplex penthouse that is rented out for private parties. It has unbelievable views and offers a stark contrast between modern design elements and naturalized outdoor areas. It has wooden floors and black iron staircases. Terraces are landscaped as lovely country gardens. Floor to ceiling windows and glass doors make the outside and inside feel like one continuous space.

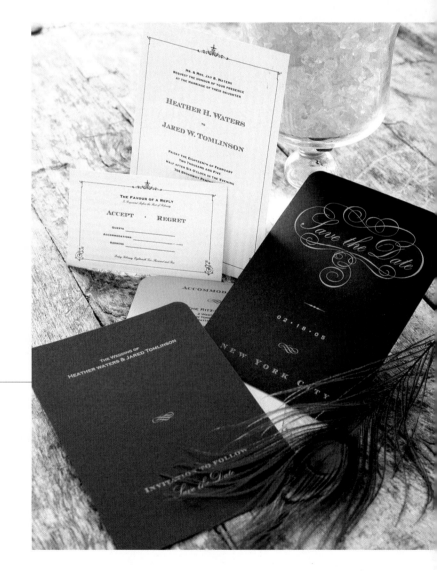

On the landing where Heather met her father, this stunning architectural arrangement of amaryllis and pussy willow made a beautiful backdrop.

When the father and bride processed toward the ceremony, their destination was a cheerful and glowing fireplace, which replaced the traditional altar. The aisle leading to it is lined on either side with aqua and white timber candles. Dramatic and sculptural, the candles are inside giant hurricane lanterns wound with pussy willow and placed atop Plexiglas cubes to elevate them farther and give them an airy, modern look. The metal urns are filled with pussy willow and orange amaryllis. Pussy willow is also woven into the urns and the lattice plinths. Votive candles lining the mantel and scattered throughout the room reflect softly in the burnished, pressed-tin ceiling.

# *Color*

## AS IMPORTANT AS THE INDIVIDUAL ELEMENTS OF MY DESIGNS ARE TO THE

*overall scheme of themes, the use of color can be so integral to The Elements that it absolutely makes them come alive, decoratively speaking. Such was very much the case here, working as we were with the icy blue of a glacier, the black-brown of bare trees, the white of snow, the orange glow of a* *briefly appearing Scandinavian winter sun. This unusual and rather stark palette worked beautifully with the wedding's sophisticated graphics, and bold strokes of color brought vibrancy to the candlelit rooms.*

*F*or the bride's bouquet we used spindly, lilylike flowers called nerines. They're very sexy and have a featherlike quality. A collar of calla lilies is surrounded by black ostrich feathers. Then we made little flowers and butterflies from guinea fowl feathers. It was really sort of *va-va-voom*.

It is only fitting for Jared that we chose a nonfloral boutonniere. He has incredible style, and a single rose just wasn't going to do the trick. How could you have va-va-voom bridesmaids' bouquets without having va-va-voom grooms-men's boutonnieres? Each boutonniere was constructed of guinea fowl feathers, pussy willow, and aqua double-faced satin ribbon bound tightly at the stem. To distinguish the groom's boutonniere we added a grouping of orange faceted crystals where the feathers met the ribbon at the neck.

For the bridesmaids we used roses and callas with champagne-colored feathers, wrapped in champagne satin ribbon. We made sure the feathers were arranged above the flowers, so they'd catch the air and flutter when the girls walked. They were very flirty and sophisticated.

As you may have surmised, the petal toss cone is one of those wedding details I love because it is such a fabulous accessory to the ceremony. Again, we used nonfloral elements, filling the cones with shimmery mica flakes and snowflake sequins. The cones themselves were aqua raw silk, which gave them a nice texture, punctuated with a beaded snowflake appliqué.

If the wedding is inside a church or ballroom, we place the petal toss cone only on aisle chairs or on the aisle ends of church pews. Many churches and locations are understandably opposed to the mess the petal toss can create, so we are willing to compromise. As long as you can create the effect without overwhelming the clean-up staff, it is much easier to manage and your photos still look amazing.

After the ceremony, guests were ushered upstairs for drinks and toasts, while the downstairs was rearranged for a buffet dinner following. After dinner, guests returned to the upstairs for music and dancing.

We worked with invitation designer Karen Bartolomei of Grapevine Weddings to create the guest book. The guest-book idea turned out to be really quite beautiful. We covered book board with a gorgeous Florentine paper and the inner pages were a mix of a light blue and aqua stock. We bound the spine with a brown-and-blue embroidered ribbon. The smaller size of this book makes it much easier to store or display.

A set of apothecary jars were appropriate for their beautiful shapes as well as for their medical connotations, a subtle nod to the bride and doctor-to-be. We filled them with all our Elements: pussy willow, blue ostrich feathers, oranges, and orange vanda orchids. Placed at one end of the bar, they were a striking alternative to flowers.

# About Food

**AS IS OFTEN THE CASE, I WORK WITH THE CATERER OR HOTEL TO HAVE THE**

menu and spirits reflect all of the design decisions we have made throughout the process. Perhaps your color palette includes pink—then pink champagne it is! The caterer for this affair was Tentation, Potel & Chabot, based in New York City. We worked closely with Nicolas Daeppen to create both savory and sweet treats that helped reinforce our design's overall look and feel. One of the passed hors d'oeuvres Nicolas chose was a Szechuan crusted tuna with coconut and sweet chili sauce on a sugar cane skewer. Not all couples want the seriousness of a full sit-down meal. Heavily passed hors d'oeuvres and stations are a great alternative for a more free-flowing evening.

On the sweeter side, we created individual white chocolate cones nestled in colored sugar (orange and blue, of course), filled with a passion fruit mousse and topped with a blueberry.

As you will see in other chapters, food can reflect not only your design but your family history and traditions. Have the chef re-create your great-grandmother's goulash, or serve your Aunt Flossie's unparalleled oatmeal cookies with after-dinner coffee.

If you are serving "finger food," particularly if it is passed, for heaven's sake make it real finger food. I hate this "super-size" trend in hors d'oeuvres. Nothing is worse than having a handful of something that is supposed to be a (tiny) mouthful—and no plate and no knife and fork. It is awkward to try to chomp something into smaller pieces and even more difficult to try to carry on a conversation while you're at it.

If you are serving dinner, keep it to two or three courses: a starter, a main course, and dessert. If you have a candy station, dessert bar, or a big-deal wedding cake, you may want to skip serving dessert at dinner. And don't make it too complicated or too much; I don't think people want to be at the table all night. They want to dance and chat. If you are so inclined, and I think it is thoughtful but not obligatory, you might ask the chef to prepare a contingency dish or two for the inevitable vegetarian or allergic-to-something guest.

*V*ery few New York apartments have pools, so we were lucky to have a pretty outside space from which to take in the views. The pool also worked with our color scheme. Here we picked up on the aqua of the water for the tablecloths. Stark winter branches combined with snowy white tulips are a vivid contrast. Twigs of pussy willow are lashed together to border the rims of simple glass vases. (That the containers are shaped like ice cubes was just a coincidence, I promise.)

# Fashion and Personal Style

## ALL BRIDES HAVE A POINT OF VIEW, DISCOVERED OR UNDISCOVERED.

What is universal is their desire to create a day uniquely their own. When I get to know a client I often find that a single idea or theme emerges as a sort of muse meant especially for that person. It may be obvious or subtle, but it is always there.

From childhood women fantasize about their weddings and the beautiful dress they will wear. The dress has an almost magical aura, and the possibility of that "once in a lifetime" gown has tremendous allure. Perhaps you have held up your mother's dress to the mirror and dreamed about your big day. It is impossible not to be moved by the sight of a bride trying on her dress for the first time—even if you're watching it in a movie. The act of helping a sister or a friend get dressed on her big day is an almost reverential ritual that touches a profound and perhaps almost primal sense of one of life's primary rites of passage.

So. How to choose the perfect dress for you? First I would say be open-minded. I can't tell you how many times I've heard a bride say, "I will never wear a poofy skirt." And the next thing you know . . . voilà: poofy skirt!

The wedding venue, location, season, and time of day set the tone of the wedding and have a great effect on the type of dress you should consider. The more formal the wedding, the more detailed or grand the dress can be. A cathedral-length train or elaborate veil is the perfect choice for an ornate church or synagogue. If your heart is set on getting married on the beach or in the backyard, perhaps a tea-length dress is more suitable.

Choose the appropriate weight fabric for the time of year. This seems obvious, but if you are trying on dresses in December for an August wedding, it might be easier to lose sight of future sweltering temperatures when you are shivering in your skivvies. Spring and summer weddings favor lightweight silks, linens, voiles, and organzas, while winter weddings comfortably accommodate heavier satins, velvets, and even fur. Whatever the season, though, the proper underpinnings are essential.

Although immensely popular, strapless dresses are not easy for every bride to wear and, if not properly fitted, may shift or slip during the course of the evening. A bride, or anyone for that matter, forced to tug at the sides of her dress for fear of wardrobe malfunction is a fashion disaster. Don't do it. Another thing to keep in mind is that bare shoulders may be frowned upon in some places of worship. If there is a question of propriety or respect for custom, the shoulders should be covered by a jacket, shawl, or veil while in the church or synagogue. (This goes for guests as well!) Afterward at the reception, there is no problem, of course.

Speaking of veils and other garments that might billow or blow, keep the weather in mind when choosing your ensemble. If you are marrying at the beach or out of doors and conditions might be windy, you don't want to be blown away—not by your dress anyway.

When you go to try on dresses, bring someone with you who knows what looks good on you. Take your time. Choosing a gown isn't much different from choosing a great cocktail dress. There are certain styles and cuts that flatter your particular figure, and you should stick with them.

There's nothing more chic than a simple gown dressed up with the right accessories. Necklaces and bracelets can change the entire appearance of a dress and are a wonderful statement of personal style.

And finally, give serious thought to your shoes and to the height of your heels. The wedding day is a long day, and nothing is worse than sore feet. Buy your shoes in advance and wear them a bit to make sure they are comfortable. And if you are going to be walking in grass or sand, make sure you can do so with the shoes you are wearing, or have someone bring along another suitable pair for after the ceremony.

With Heather it was her obsession with couture and her enthusiasm for fashion that probably pulled me the most. The first thing she did was show me Polaroids of her dress. She didn't feel like we could go forward until I saw the dress and her accessories—a feather boa, a fur, a crystal necklace—which she planned to change throughout the evening. To her, my understanding of her fashion sense would greatly enhance the creative process. And it did. The cuff of ostrich feathers in her bouquet and the feather butterflies and flowers could all just as easily have been stitched onto a ball gown. Not every bride has the confidence to allow such an unusual and elaborate bouquet, fearing it might distract from her dress (and therefore from her). But it was right for Heather, and she could carry it off.

We have had grooms in their traditional family tartan kilts and in their crisp U.S. Coast Guard dress whites. Weddings offer so many opportunities to express your personal style through fashion. Make creative decisions that do reflect who you are and what you are about.

If you are going to the expense of giving gifts to each guest, it should be something that is meaningful and representative in some way of the day. The bride's grandfather contributed the old family recipe for glogg, a Swedish specialty drink to warm the coldest of winter chills. Heavy craft paper boxes were filled with glogg cups and a tin of ingredient spices, trimmed in embroidered ribbon. To make it more of a keepsake, we added recipe cards tacked to the inside of the lid.

There is something particularly romantic about a winter wedding, and all the more so with New York City as the backdrop. Sky Studios was a setting that offered an unusual combination of urban hipness and congenial intimacy, well-suited to a couple whose modern sensibilities and keen fashion sense were tempered by their family closeness and respect for heritage. Through the Elements of design throughout the ceremony, dinner, and dancing to the wee hours, guests were able to see and experience what Heather and Jared loved and valued, and to understand that they, too, as friends and family, were very much a part of that.

### GLÖGG

4 (750 ML) BOTTLES OF PORT WINE
1 (750 ML) BOTTLE OF WHISKEY
1 LARGE ORANGE – CUT INTO CUBES
1 SPICE BAG (CONTAINING 24 WHOLE CLOVES AND 6 CINNAMON STICKS)
*hint: use either a big tea ball or a white cloth tied together with string*
1 CUP OF RAISINS, 1 CUP OF BLANCHED ALMONDS, 1 CUP OF SUGAR

Place liquid and spice bag in pan and simmer for 15 minutes. After the first 15 minutes add 1 cup raisins, 1 cup blanched almonds and 1 cup sugar. Simmer for another 15 minutes or so. Taste to see if it is spiced enough. If not let simmer awhile longer with spices in. Take out spice bag and let cool. Taste once again to see if sweetness is good. If not add more sugar to taste. Serve Glogg hot with a few raisins and almonds in the bottom of a small glass.
**ENJOY AND SKOAL TO ALL!!**

# It's About Time, It's About Space

**DECIDING WHAT SORT OF AMBIENCE YOU WANT TO CREATE IN YOUR** ceremony and reception is important in choosing where to hold them. The church- or synagogue-and-club combo has become a standard because it is always appropriate and therefore removes a certain amount of stress in the planning stages. But "standard" may not be your thing, as it was not with Heather and Jared.

For them, having the ceremony and reception in the same place—Sky Studios in New York—worked because it felt like one big cocktail party from beginning to end, exactly what Heather said she wanted. What's spectacular about this location is that it does feel like home, albeit a grand one. Sky Studios also has remarkable architecture, so that when the guests move from one part of the space to another there is something new to discover. Continuity helps maintain the energy level, while changing settings holds the interest. That's also part of the challenge.

After the ceremony, guests were ushered upstairs for cocktails while downstairs was transformed into a giant living room. Since Heather wasn't having a traditional seated meal, we decorated with leather sofas, club chairs, and small round tables, like in a nightclub. Then we added throw pillows and tons of candles. When the guests returned for dinner, the space had been totally transformed. It was like magic (with a lot of work).

If a room is going to serve double duty, make sure your caterer and florist have enough staff for the "flip," or changeover of the room. Taking down a chuppah and setting dinner tables is a highly orchestrated affair that requires both muscle and organization to pull off successfully and smoothly.

The other tricky part about a single location is moving guests from one place to another without the use of a cattle prod. I think what takes the frustration out of it is the level of service you create. A well-trained staff should greet each guest personally and invite him or her to dinner, and offer to carry the drinks to the table, at least the ladies' drinks anyway. There are always the die-hards who don't want to leave their bourbons even for a second, but most of the time people are ready. It's all about the human touch. I've also used everything from strolling musicians to stilt walkers to persuade guests into the next room.

Another way to move the party along is to have the bride and groom invite the guests themselves. Because they are usually delayed with taking photographs after the ceremony, the newlyweds don't always make it to cocktails immediately following. So it's exciting for everyone when they make an entrance and announce, "Dinner is served."

Seashells and Bahamian Chic

With its pristine pink sand beaches, pastel cottages, and palm trees, Harbour Island is about as idyllic a setting for a wedding as you could have. Accessible only by boat, the tiny Bahamian enclave keeps a slow and steady pace. Motorized transportation consists of scooters and golf carts, which are perfectly adequate to navigate the island's rabbit warren of streets winding through all of its three or so square miles. There is no Starbucks, no Club Cinquante-Cinq. Life in the little Caribbean community revolves around the sea and simple pleasures.

But as laid back as it is, it's also very chic, with such stylish habitués as the late designer David Hicks, his daughter India, supermodel Elle Macpherson, and, I have to say, our bride, Maggie. So chic and with an incredible sense of style, Maggie is fashion-forward and fearless, and was a wonderful partner in designing this wedding.

Raised in Wisconsin in a house by a lake, Maggie grew up loving the water. So Harbour Island was a natural enough choice for a holiday. But little did she know she would find it, as she says, "the most charming place in the world." She fell in love with the island immediately and knew it was the place she wanted to have her wedding some day.

When she met her next great love, Steve, it wasn't long before she lured him to this most charming place, and both agreed in time to be married there.

What made this wedding so special, though, was that it wasn't just *on* Harbour Island, it was *of* Harbour Island, which is important. The boys' choir "introduced" the arrival of the rehearsal dinner guests with spirited singing, while the local gospel choir sang during the ceremony. A native *Junkanoo* band played and led the newlyweds and guests from the church to the reception. The flavor lent spice to Maggie's sophisticated and elegant taste, and the couple's implicit respect for the spirit of the island not only enhanced the occasion but enriched everyone's experience of it.

## Season:

Mid-spring

## Setting:

Harbour Island, Bahamas

## Situation:

A destination wedding with about 150 invited guests. An intimate rehearsal dinner was held for family and wedding party only, while others were invited to a cocktail party. The ceremony was held in a small island chapel; the reception under a tent at the Rock House.

## Ideas and Inspirations

| | | | | | | | |
|---|---|---|---|---|---|---|---|
| THE SEA | THE SEA | THE SEA | WAVES | BOATS | SAILING | SEASHELLS | SEA CREATURES |
| SEA HORSES | BARNACLES | WATER | BLUE | AQUA | SUNSHINE | SAND | SEA URCHINS |
| BUBBLES | PINK SAND | CORAL | RIBBON | MAPS | PALE BLUE | PEONIES | CHANDELIER EARRINGS |
| JEWELRY | ORCHIDS | MUSIC | WIND CHIMES | BLUE | TEXTURE | STRIKING | FASHION |

# The Elements

# *The Elements*

## SHELLS

I am obsessed with all things from the sea, and I marvel every time I look at a shell. If you take the time to see it, each one is like a Sistine Chapel. One of the most beautiful experiences of my life was, as a child, walking along the beach at the Jersey shore after a storm. There were thousands, and I mean thousands, of conch shells. It was magical. We used shells everywhere for this wedding. Like charms, they work well as accessories or accents.

## SEA HORSES

Endearing and architectural, the sea horse became a sort of emblem for the entire design of the wedding. The invitations, the decorations, even the gift bags were engraved, embossed, glued, or embroidered with these charming little creatures. And what do you know? They mate for life.

## SEA URCHINS

I'm always looking for a fresh approach to the things we see around us, and funnily enough, the bride's jewelry was my inspiration for this choice of Element and how we interpreted it. Maggie is never without a pair of beautiful chandelier earrings. Sea urchins, in all their colors and sizes, lent themselves beautifully to being strung like beads dangling like jewelry in the Bahamian breeze.

## THE SEA

As I've said, on a three-mile-long island it is futile to try to ignore the sparkling aquamarine waters surrounding it. So for this wedding the sea was the Element that informed almost every design decision we made. From the shells to the barnacles, to the sea urchins, to the fabric and, above all, the colors, the sea was our constant guide. It was also quite the gathering place. On the morning we were shooting on the beach, five horses appeared, rolled in the sand, and proceeded to amble right by where we were working. It was amazing.

## GIANT BARNACLES

I know, I know, barnacles are an unlikely choice, but their multiple colors and strong sculptural shapes make them beautiful to work with. Shipping fresh flowers to some Caribbean islands is very difficult, and shells and hard goods are an excellent and beautiful alternative. The giant barnacles mixed with big chunky shells and bunches of flowers became a base design Element in some cases and stood on their own in others. They are incredibly unusual and very striking.

## The Colors

TURQUOISE

ROBIN'S EGG

CORAL

SHELL PINK

## The Details

Welcome friends and family! Gift bags are an important component of the destination wedding, and these were very popular, in white and bright green canvas and embroidered with sea horses. Tucked in every one was an accordion-folded welcome note and a handmade mini-guidebook with a schedule and details of the weekend's activities as well as helpful information about the island itself. Beginning your weekend on such a thoughtful, fun note as this instantly puts your guests in a festive spirit.

While a destination wedding does limit your options, I found Harbour Island's little pink church to be perfect. For Maggie, however, it was a point of concern because she feared it was too plain. True, unlike more architecturally elaborate houses of worship, this one could stand a little embellishment. So rather than do the typical two flower arrangements on the altar, we sought to create a really beautiful entrance. We accented the pillars flanking the door with arrangements of giant barnacles, amaryllis, and roses, trailing white ribbon streamers with sea horses and shells. Just above this we created oval lush pink rose sconces with shell medallions for "lights."

For the program box and the programs we covered a simple wooden box with aqua silk and wrapped the box with ribbon and medium-size shells and sea urchins. It almost looks like a piece of jewelry and makes a wonderful keepsake once the festivities are over. The programs themselves are hand-bound by pale blue ribbon in a crisscross pattern—labor intensive, but oh, so elegant.

The programs were closely linked in design to Maggie and Steve's invitations, which were white with silver engraving, overlaid with a vellum map and tucked into a woven cuff of silky pale blue ribbon. They were mailed in pale blue envelopes with white calligraphy. I absolutely love white calligraphy, and I love it when the papery is a continuous design statement—perhaps because it is one of a wedding's most beautiful keepsakes. (For more on papery, see page 186.)

We had a lot of fun with the "flowers" on this wedding, because so many of them weren't. Small cone shells wound with copper jewelry wire accented the tiny, fragrant stephanotis flowers for the boutonnieres. The color of the copper wire accentuates the coral color of the groomsmen's shirts and plays well against their navy jackets. Stephanotis grows wild on the island and also was used for the wreaths the flower girls wore in their hair.

The little girls loved their wreaths, but they went bananas when they got their flower buckets. Little aluminum buckets covered in silk and trimmed in ribbon with woven ribbon handles were glued with colorful shells and sea horses and filled with roses the color of the pink sandy beaches. These mighty little buckets encompass all of the design Elements and also pop against their creamy organza dresses.

For the bridesmaids, coral was the perfect accent color. Not only is it named for a product of the sea, it is complementary to blue in the color wheel. (Its paler shade in the groomsmen's shirts echoed the famous Harbour Island pink sands, which are in fact crushed coral.) Spray roses, ranunculus, sweet pea, and shells are bound together with a ribbon cuff and seashell insignia.

Maggie's favorite flower is the peony, and that is what she had her heart set on for her bouquet. But shipping peonies to the Caribbean, yikes. As it turns out, peonies are very hardy and recover beautifully once cut and popped into a cooler for a day or two, so peonies it was.

For Maggie's bouquet we mixed in some white cymbidiums to give it a tropical touch. The stems are tightly wrapped in French-braided satin ribbon with pearl pins between each twist to give it a bit of a couture feel. We chose a more composed shape for the bouquet as not to fight the lace of Maggie's dress and the fashion-forward jewelry she chose.

# Island Apparel and Other Considerations

## ISLAND WEDDINGS ARE WARM, ROMANTIC, AND PICTURESQUE, OH YES.

They can also be windy, humid, and hot. You needn't be daunted, but you do need to be dressed and groomed appropriately—no pun intended! Starting from the top down, work with your hairstylist and makeup person to determine a look that will hold up under the elements and that you will not have to fuss with every time the photographer strolls by. Share this info with your bridesmaids, mother, groom's mother, and friends. You and your bridesmaids might even make an outing of it and have a salon day as the wedding approaches. Or you might make arrangements with a local salon to help you out in this department. And if you haven't learned this yet, please learn it now: No amount of great hair or makeup can ever completely conceal a sunburn and nothing looks worse in photos, so keep your hat on at all times and don't spare the sunscreen.

For your wedding gown and bridesmaids' dresses, choose fabrics that are light and breezy (no duchesse satin), but in styles that won't flap and fly all over the place. Maggie chose a gorgeous dress that picked up the breezes perfectly. She chose not to wear a veil, as they are unpredictable at best when the wind kicks up, and that the wind will kick up is predictable.

I am guessing that if you are an island-beachy kind of girl you can get along at least for a little while without your three-inch Jimmy Choos. Sand, rocks, and erratically paved roads are no place for stilettos. Choose a pretty, strappy sandal or a delicate slipper sort of shoe with no or a low heel—or proceed at your own risk.

As for the men, be merciful and choose suits or blazers that don't have them sweating bullets throughout the ceremony and reception. They'll be miserable and will look it in the pictures. Little boys look adorable in shorts, and personally I think little boys should be dressed like little boys anyway and not like little men.

aving set the tone at the church with the arrangements outside the entrance, we wanted to create an even more remarkable welcome to the reception. One of the charming things about Harbour Island is all its tiny side streets, but it does make many of its buildings inconspicuous and rather hard to find. The two lanterns flanking the Rock House entrance became the basis for our "chandelier earring" mobile constructions, with their tops encrusted with giant barnacles and shells, and the delicately strung sea urchins and shells drifting down from there. The light illuminated the shells to great effect as they dangled and danced in the evening breeze. And all of a sudden the entrance wasn't so inconspicuous anymore. Don Purdy and Wallace Tutt, the owners of the Rock House, were so delighted with the shell mobiles they asked us to leave them behind! It makes me smile to imagine them still fluttering in the breeze.

93

The seating card table is a chance to create a real zinger of a centerpiece in the area where guests have cocktails before dinner. It is one of the first things guests interact with and it's an opportunity to be a bit playful, if the mood is light and the atmosphere relaxed, as it very much was in our idyllic island setting.

One thing to keep in mind, however, as with any outdoor setting and particularly by the ocean: the wind. We met this challenge with a Plexiglas stand with little shelves, and filled the shelves with that beautiful Bahamian pink sand. The pearlized blue cards nestled right in and didn't blow away. But then we also had to deal with the stand itself, which we bolted right onto the table. Shells, barnacles, and a scattering of orchids covered the base of the stand and the table. We couldn't resist hot gluing sea horses onto Plexiglas cubes and scattering them among the shells at the base. This way they were sure to not get lost in the shells and gave the design more dimension. And, of course, the shimmery blue envelopes and cards themselves were also beautiful, with kissing sea horses blind-embossed on white museum board and silver calligraphy.

For the cocktail table arrangements we took a simple approach, filling a blue glass vase with colorful Haitian tree snails, cymbidium orchids, and more shells, the last wired with wooden flower pics to be easily inserted into the arrangement.

# On Outdoor Weddings

## RULE NUMBER ONE FOR PLANNING AN OUTDOOR WEDDING IS TO PLAN AN

*indoor wedding as a backup. If I've learned anything it is that Plan B is as critical as Plan A. Weather is one of the few things a wedding designer cannot control, but that does not mean we cannot prepare for it.*

*Whether there is a tent or not, I am a huge believer in flooring. Going barefoot on the beach is one thing, and a fun thing, but apart from that no lady wants to have her heels sink into the ground, let alone have her shoes soiled irreparably.*

*Make sure you have proper ventilation and heating or cooling if called for. Heating is not a bank breaker, but air conditioning a tent is expensive. Depending on the size of the tent it can be anywhere from $5,000 to $10,000 and up. Make sure the property or house has enough power to supply your electrical needs, otherwise spring for a generator. It's the best $1,500 you'll spend.*

*Other elements of nature must be contended with as well, including nature's calls. Not all portable restrooms are created equal. Try to find a company that has the portable bathrooms in trailers, with half sinks and other amenities. And do remember to dress these up a bit with flowers, inexpensive rugs perhaps, and baskets of amenities. Hire attendants, if you can, to keep them stocked and tidy.*

*If it rains, have umbrellas on hand to move guests from place to place. Have a car on reserve for the bride to take her to the ceremony, and perhaps reserve cars for wedding party, wedding couple's parents, and other family members or friends, particularly the elderly. Provide baskets of shawls if it might turn chilly, or have fans on hand if the temperature rises.*

For a sitting area the guests passed through on their way from cocktails to dinner, we did a bit of a show-off thing with Maggie's favorite peonies, roses, tulips, orchids, and stars-of-Bethlehem in a shell-encrusted vase, lit by shell-studded mosaic hurricane lanterns.

And for the dinner itself, we worked very closely with owners Don and Wallace to pull the right team together and execute the final design. As is often the case in destination weddings, those who are there day in and day out can truly make or break your day. As with all larger dinners at the Rock House, the swimming pool is covered with Plexiglas, so the guests could dance over water. Turquoise and white paper bubble lanterns floated above the surface and palm trees swayed in the distance. We had silver ballroom chairs brought in by container ship from Florida, as the standard white wood folding chairs just weren't going to have the effect we wanted.

The tables are draped in a gorgeous aqua, pale blue, and white striped silk dupioni floor-length linen. White bisque vases resembling the shape of sea cucumbers are the perfect vessels for dinner table centerpieces, as are clear glass sea urchin shapes and white bisque sea urchin votives. Flowers are cymbidiums, stars-of-Bethlehem, spray roses, and peonies. Each place setting is adorned with a single cymbidium flower over crisp white linen dinner napkins.

# About
# Destination Weddings

## SOMEONE ONCE SAID TO ME (I BELIEVE IT WAS MY GRANDMOTHER), WHEN

you are faced with something you can't avoid, lean into it. This is both the blessing and the curse of the so-called destination wedding: that some aspect of the design almost necessarily has to be about the destination. Otherwise, why go? The blessing of the destination wedding is that some of your most obvious design elements are built in. The curse is that those elements are, well, obvious. And you want to be original.

Don't let the fact that "it's all been done before" discourage you. Trust me, everything has been done before. And trust me again, there is a way to make it uniquely your own. In our Harbour Island setting, it was all about the sea and there was just no getting away from it—especially not on a three-mile-long piece of land. But that did not mean there weren't waves of good ideas. Seashells, sea horses, and a cool Caribbean blue palette are simple conceptually but extremely versatile. I always look for unusual ways to apply what may be not-so-unusual design elements, like shell "buttons" on ribbon cuffs for the bridesmaids' bouquets, and "chandeliers" (Maggie's favorite earring choice) of sea urchins, and giant barnacles as bases for floral arrangements. In other words, go with what is there, and think of using it in different ways. Just because something is conventional does not mean it is cliché.

So, as you may have gathered, I don't think it's enough just to book a resort and hire a caterer. A destination wedding should embrace the spirit of the place. Learn what the local customs and traditions are and incorporate some of them into your celebration. Find out what the regional specialties are in everything from food to dress, and pick up on the aspects that appeal to you. Maggie and Steve having the local gospel choir in their ceremony, the Junkanoo band following, and a steel band at the reception not only amused and entertained the guests but gave the festivities a soulful and authentic cultural

context. Remember that destination weddings require a considerable effort not only on the part of the hosts but also of the guests, who may have traveled great distances and rung up great Amex bills in honor of your big day. So it is nice for them to feel they have really been somewhere.

As a practical matter, destination weddings require more formal and written communication than a wedding closer to home, so the paper products take on greater importance, from the save-the-date card to, in Maggie and Steve's case, an accordion-folded welcome note with details of the weekend's festivities as well as tips on getting around the island.

Mail your save-the-date six to eight months in advance so that people can block out the time in their schedule. The second mailing would be the wedding invitation, but mail these a bit in advance of the standard three to four weeks; I recommend six to eight weeks. A third mailing should go out closer to the event, about three weeks ahead, with advice on what clothes to bring, schedule of activities, spa appointments, tee times, and so forth.

Depending on the location, you may want to organize group activities. For this wedding, the guys went sailing and the girls sat on the beach and then had lunch at an adorable seaside restaurant called Sip Sip. Other options might be lunch and an afternoon at the spa, a chartered fishing trip, or a sunset sailing cruise. In most cases, these activities will need to be booked in advance, so give guests a card or form on which to indicate their choices when they respond to the wedding invitation. If the event or activity is not to be paid for by the bride or groom's family, indicate on the response card the approximate cost involved so your guests are prepared. I find this perfectly acceptable, by the way.

You may also want to reserve on-island transportation to ensure your guests don't find themselves stranded. Harbour

Island is particularly small and golf carts are the mode of transport. Through the hotel the couple reserved fifty golf carts. As you can see I picked up a hitchhiker who stuck with me for most of the day while I whizzed around checking on details.

Keep in mind, however, that you do not have to schedule every minute of your guests' time. In most cases your guests will be combining your ceremony with a holiday, and the event should not feel like a forced march. When people travel to a destination wedding, they appreciate having time to pursue their own interests.

Do have a welcome packet or a gift bag. The packet should include a note from the couple thanking them for coming, as well as practical information such as maps, a list of restaurants, points of interest, shopping info, and suggested activities. Make sure your gift is thoughtful and something your guests would want. Don't burden them with something

they would rather not have to carry home. It can also be fun to organize with housekeeping to leave a small treat for each guest at night. It might be a small trinket or keepsake, or perhaps an invitation to the next day's activity.

If there are to be children present, make accommodations for them. You may want to bring down a nanny or two to care for children during the adult-only events. You may want to organize a children's reception or work with the property to arrange a special event for them. Movie night can be a very popular option, for example. It is also all right to make it known that children are not invited to the wedding. Just be aware that you will be eliminating people if you make this decision.

Whatever you do, be sure to have some sort of opening gathering so that all the guests can begin to meet each other. This is an excellent opportunity for close friends or relatives other than the bride's or groom's immediate families who want to contribute something to the wedding weekend by hosting a cocktail party, brunch or luncheon, or a sporting or cultural outing. In these cases, those hosting that particular event would send the invitation and be responsible for organizing it. It also gives the people responsible for the wedding a small break and can add a different flavor to the events.

A destination wedding is its own adventure and takes incredible dedication on the part of everyone involved. For that reason a real sense of camaraderie is generated among the hosts and the guests alike. Like a big project they've all been working on together, these very special and increasingly popular weddings are great fun and especially memorable.

The bride and groom's chairs are draped in double-faced satin ribbon hot glued with sea horses and framed by sea urchin streamers, which had the subtle effect of soft wind chimes whenever Maggie or Steve moved their chairs—the sweet music of beautiful memories in the making.

Maggie and Steve created a magical night. Their guests "rocked the house" and danced the night away. Nobody was ready for the night to end. . . . Now, that's when you know after three days of being together you have created the perfect night.

Jennie Rabinowitz and Daniel Jamieson met at Wesleyan University in Middletown, Connecticut, and were cordial acquaintances their first two years. But the summer after their sophomore year, everything changed. As Jennie tells it, she was interning at The Institute for Unpopular Culture and studying Arabic in preparation for spending her junior year in Morocco. Dan was taking a psychology course and scooping ice cream at Ben & Jerry's. Jennie was living in a less-than-desirable apartment on a block with two sausage factories under a highway overpass in San Francisco. Dan, on the other hand, had "a critter-free Berkeley abode." Jennie says she began spending as much time at Dan's as possible. Jennie and Dan were assigned the same dorm, on the same hall, at Wesleyan, and the romance continued to blossom.

Northern California, with its heart-stoppingly beautiful forests and craggy coastline, was heaven for Jennie and Dan, who spent much of their time together hiking, fishing, and camping during summer breaks. Their love of the outdoors inspired their love for each other and continues to this day. After Wesleyan, both remained on the East Coast, Jennie to law school in New York, Dan to medical school in Boston, later moving to New York to complete his residency. In summers they love going to Maine and visiting friends who own a working farm there. In addition to pitching in with the farm chores, Jennie and Dan still love hiking amid the towering pines and cedars, and they eat lots of lobster and blueberry pie. The two were a couple for eight years before they married, but their ardor for the outdoors, and for each other, never cooled.

If it were left to Jennie, she would probably just as soon have gotten married in a meadow. Her mother had other ideas, however. The closest thing to a meadow near New York's St. Regis Hotel was the Sheep Meadow in Central Park. And now for not the first time, I am presented with the challenge of designing a wedding to suit two seemingly very different styles. But, as is often the case with mothers and brides, their tastes ultimately are entirely reconcilable. (Thank goodness.)

*I* do have to ask, what is not to love about a wedding at The St. Regis? The fabled Fifth Avenue institution has hosted the weddings of some of New York's—and the world's—most glamorous stars and socialites, and their service is absolutely unparalleled. Working there is a dream. I knew we could find a way to incorporate Jennie and Dan's love of the outdoors with Jennie's mother's love of classic elegance. In fact Jennie and her mother shared a very similar aesthetic; it is just that they came at it from two different points of view. What seemed to make it all work was keeping with the classics.

### Season:

Late summer

### Setting:

Ceremony and dinner reception at The St. Regis Hotel in Manhattan

### Situation:

A formal evening wedding with a traditional Jewish ceremony. About two hundred guests will attend the ceremony and seated dinner following. Design aims to please different tastes of mother and daughter by incorporating as many natural and outdoorsy elements as possible into a classic, formal setting.

## Ideas and Inspirations

| | | | | | | | |
|---|---|---|---|---|---|---|---|
| BLUEBERRIES | BOHEMIAN | BLACK TIE | FISHING | ROCKS | WROUGHT IRON | OLD GATES | CAMPING |
| RETRO | LOVE FOR THE OUTDOORS | MEADOWS | GARDENS | CANDLELIGHT | SUMMER | MAINE | BLUE |
| GREEN | | HYDRANGEA | BERRIES | FOREST | COASTLINES | NORTHERN CALIFORNIA | HIKING |

## BERRIES

There are lots of good growing things that aren't flowers, and berries are one of them. Sweet, lush, plump, juicy, wild, cultivated, abundant. Blueberries have full-on summer foliage and are a bright chartreuse before they ripen into that deep purply blue, so they suited our color palette perfectly. They also suited the bride, as a strong but subtle acknowledgment of her passion for the outdoors and barefoot summer mornings. The smaller, dark purple berries are viburnum berries, a nice contrast to the chartreuse of the unripe blueberry, and a complement to the dusty blue of the ripe one.

## RIVER ROCKS

Representing both earth and water, river rocks were the perfect Element to bring the outdoors in, and they were a beautiful complement to the marble architectural elements and furnishings of the hotel, particularly the fireplace and the marble-topped consoles in the hallway leading from the ceremony to the reception. And the idea of using stones in the garden—for paths and coping—was another nice fit with our theme.

## HYDRANGEA

Hydrangeas are a favorite of Jennie's and of mine. They are such wonderful, gardeny flowers and in full bloom in midsummer, which was perfect for us. Also because it was summer and we were inside, I wanted to dispel any kind of a cooped-up feeling. Vibrant colors create a sense of movement and freshness. Jennie loved blue and green and never wavered from her choices, reflecting as they do the Northern Californian coastline. Combining the deep purply-blue hydrangea with vivid shades of green and chartreuse is an electric combination and looked great against all the gilt and crystal of the St. Regis ballroom.

## WROUGHT IRON

For both its design and its craftsmanship, the Element of decorative ironwork became an obvious choice when I saw Jennie's invitation. It was the perfect Element to tie in a garden theme with a classic look and to make it pretty and dressy but not overly formal. The disciplined forms and curves lend themselves easily to decorative motifs in everything from the urns holding flower arrangements to the wedding program design.

## The Colors

HYDRANGEA BLUE

BLUEBERRY

CHARTREUSE

PERIWINKLE

## The Details

Funnily enough, it was the invitation that provided our strongest creative point of departure, and Jennie had already chosen it by the time she came to me. Its classical scroll-like motif reminded me of decorative wrought ironwork and beautiful garden gates. And there it was, our inspiration! And a garden theme was certainly appropriate for late summer. But best of all it gave us the outdoorsy component Jennie craved combined with the more formal, dressy element her mother sought. Like Jennie and Dan, it was a perfect match. Though Jennie had chosen her invitation from Peculiar Pair Press before she came to me, I include it here because it became a creative touchstone for us, inspiring the garden theme and the design of the remaining papery.

109

A lovely St. Regis touch, tea sandwiches and petits fours were prepared for the bridal party as they dressed for the ceremony in their luxurious suite, knowing dinner was still a ways off.

# Hotel Weddings

**HOTEL WEDDINGS ARE WONDERFUL BECAUSE THEY ARE ALMOST COMPLETELY**

controllable environments—unlike outdoor weddings or tented receptions. Once you negotiate your package, the facilities, food and drinks, and guest rooms, if any, you know exactly what you're dealing with financially. (I tell brides who are having a tented affair in their backyards to add 40 percent to their expected budgets and they'll be closer to the real number.) Another positive aspect of hotel weddings is that you are working with an experienced and organized group of pros who

know how it's done. As a first-time bride, your biggest challenge may be that "you don't know what you don't know," and a seasoned hotel banquet manager has an arsenal of solutions at his or her fingertips to solve almost any problem.

I am personally in love with working at the St. Regis in New York City. Their attention to detail and top-notch service is worth every penny—and they have great food, too!

*I*t was important to the bride that the wedding program appropriately reflect the tone of the occasion—a festive celebration but a religious ceremony as well, and a sacred rite. The program also included a note of thanks and appreciation from the couple to their families and friends, and a remembrance of loved ones who were no longer with them. For the program's design I was inspired by the beautiful damask on the walls of the St. Regis hallways, and by the elaborate metal grates reaching from floor to ceiling that are remnants of the hotel's old forced-air cooling system. Of course, this brings in our ironwork element as well. Again working with The Wedding Library by Claudia Hanlin and Jennifer Zabinski, we picked Ceci to create the wedding program. It was printed with a damask pattern to mimic the metalwork designs and paired with a chocolate-brown liner paper. The text pages were cream with chocolate-brown ink.

For the chuppah, we covered a wooden platform base with fern-green fabric and draped the canopy and posts in white organza, which is light, summery, and bridal, but not too poofy or frothy. At the base of the posts are bright white hydrangeas, and at either side are large floor-standing arrangements of Casablanca lilies, white snowball hydrangeas, Polo roses, and pear branches in handsome iron urns. Then we created a waterfall of candlelight in front of the mirror by suspending votives with fishing line. The fishing line is practically invisible, so the candles appear to float, and the groom was happy about that as he is an avid fisherman.

At the entrance to the Versailles Room where the ceremony was held, neat rows of gold ballroom chairs were divided by an aisle marked with four-foot-high iron candelabras and a pair of large standing arrangements similar to those at the chuppah. A program was placed on each chair.

*R*eversing the customary color choice, we gave the bride a colorful bouquet and gave the bridesmaids all white. Here, we have chartreuse and blue hydrangea, heleboris, sage, tweedia, and a seed-pod-looking thing called diplocyclos. The wrapping is an electric blue, double-faced satin secured with a "button" of diplocyclos. The small blue tweedia flowers are an apt choice for this particular outdoorsy bride because they remind me of meadow flowers.

*F*or the boutonnieres, tiny tweedia blossoms punctuated by the diplocyclos pods and wrapped in chartreuse satin looked beautiful against the groomsmen's dinner jackets. The twiggy tendrils of the diplocyclos gave the boutonnieres a woodsy effect.

Along the grand marble hallway leading from the Versailles Room to the cocktail reception in the Library were two imposing marble consoles that we simply but dramatically decorated with varying heights of glass cylinders filled with white river rocks, water, and floating candlelight. The river rocks enhance the texture and patina of the marble, while the candlelight danced in its own reflection from the water, walls, and tabletops. There wasn't a flower in sight and it could not have been more effective.

Again taking our cue from the invitation and its scroll-work, we execute the garden gate idea quite literally for the seating card table. We rented this lovely gate from a New York prop house and wove it with jasmine—a beautiful summer flower with an intoxicating aroma. Beneath it is the seating card table on which we had woven a lattice grid of twigs, which propped up the seating cards nicely. We let the jasmine vines trail along the table. With every design choice we made, we tried to bring in as many natural elements as possible to give Jennie the garden wedding she desired. Upon entering the room you really felt as if you were entering a garden. This one knocked people out.

If you are having a seated dinner, the seating card table should be the first thing the guests see as they come into cocktails after the ceremony, so it is very important visually. I tend to like them to be three-dimensional, because I find a single flat expanse of cards can be a bit boring. But beyond that I also like to create a sense of destination about the table.

In lieu of a formal *placement* with individual place cards and the almost inevitable last-minute drama of revisions, additions, and subtractions, an excellent option is to give guests table assignments and to leave it at that. This allows you to assemble the group and lets them work out their seats. It's a flexible approach and therefore very well-suited to larger crowds and less formal affairs.

The Library was considerately furnished with small round tables skirted in white linen with a broad lime green cuff and gold ballroom chairs whose lattice-design backs were in good keeping with our garden theme. On the tables are small white iron urns holding white lisianthus and star-of-Bethlehem, with river rocks scattered at their bases. Flanking the massive hearth are tall metal urns holding snowball hydrangeas and good old Boston fern, which fit with the Victorian feeling of the room. And as everyone knows, the Victorians were great lovers of gardens and flowers.

From cocktails, guests were invited upstairs for dinner and dancing in the storied St. Regis ballroom with its soaring barrel-vaulted ceiling replete with painted clouds and frolicking puti, swoops and swags of curtains, and crystal chandeliers and sconces as far as the eye can see. How to approach such a space without being overwhelmed by it? We kept it fresh and simple and let the room add the glamour. Remaining true to our color scheme, tablecloths are periwinkle silk dupioni with a chartreuse cuff (echoing the cocktail tablecloths). The centerpieces, some in low, classically shaped iron urns and some mounted on tall wrought-iron candle stands, held compositions of blue Dutch hydrangea, kangaroo paws, lisianthus, bella donna and bella mosa, Super Green roses, viburnum berry, and blueberry.

Napkins are another mighty little design component. Napkins can add a splash of color, house the dinner menu, or become the canvas or backdrop for a flower or other decorative flourish. We often have them made to order. These in particular were green on one side and blue on the other. The pillar candles were given chartreuse satin ribbon cuffs, pulling the tablescape together very neatly.

# About Centerpieces

## THE CENTERPIECE IS THE CROWNING JEWEL OF YOUR DINNER RECEPTION

*and the first thing guests look for when entering the room. Although there are many elements that tie the décor of the room together, the centerpiece is the heart of the design.*

*Centerpieces can take so many forms. They can be composed or loose and flowy. They can have single flower notes, or a mix of many. My design director, Kim Hirst, and I spend many hours in the flower market researching each season's bounty to think of new ways to incorporate texture and complexity into every centerpiece we create. It is Kim's theory that it should be so beautiful you almost want to eat it.*

*If the centerpiece is the lead, it has many supporting actors. The container or vessel you choose has great influence on the finished design. Often we create smaller satellite arrangements surrounding the main centerpiece to give the table more substance.*

*But, of course, none of it matters if you cannot see it. Candlelight from above and below makes flowers glow, and pin spotlights from the ceiling almost make your centerpiece jump off the table visually.*

Aside from the color of the vases, the menu cards were the one other element on the dinner table that lightened things up a bit. The menus were printed on cream stock with the letterpressed gate pattern both at the top of the interior page of the menu and spine of the exterior cover.

The cake was designed by Cheryl Kleinman, with a clean, simple look and a slightly retro feel, a style the bride herself gravitated toward. It was very much a classic but with this subtle sort of retro edge. Palm fronds and small flowers were an outdoorsy touch, while a shimmery icing finish made it soft and feminine and elegant. (Lemon pound cake with lemon buttercream and raspberry filling, by the way, with marzipan icing—yum!) Cheryl makes stunning cakes with remarkable attention to detail.

# Working with Wedding Planners

**WEDDING PLANNERS ARE AN ASSET FOR ANY BRIDE WHO IS WORKING FULL-TIME**

*and is planning a large-scale wedding or a destination wedding. Remember that once the wedding weekend arrives you want to be a worry-free bride. The wedding planner facilitates and becomes the liaison between all parties, including the bride and her family, the designer, the caterer, and all the vendors. The planner is the perfect partner to the bride and runs interference for her every step of the way. A wedding planner can become the bride's eyes and ears and spare the bride and her parents the myriad of little questions that must be answered but not necessarily by them. He or she can help with travel arrangements, checking deliveries, dealing with the band or other entertainment, accommodating last-minute guests at seated dinners (horror!), and just troubleshooting in general. Something always comes up, and I have a saying for it: "You don't know what you don't know." I say let the wedding planner figure it out, and let the bride enjoy being a bride.*

From sweets to sweet dreams, they do a beautiful turn-down service at the St. Regis. Here a hydrangea and rose petal heart on the blanket cover is a thoughtful and romantic decorative gesture and a fitting close to a dream of a wedding. The winning combination of a dedicated and creative team allowed the bride and her mother each to express her own preferences and style to find the perfect marriage of elegance and ease.

*Equine and Confectionary*

$\mathscr{L}$ong before they discovered a passion for each other, Brendan Cassidy and Adele Sessa shared a passion for horses. Both ride, train, and teach. Both own and operate horse farms. Both in New Jersey. Both allow only black-and-white cats around their barns, if you can believe that. And both have an absolute love of sweets, because both of their grandparents owned candy stores! How could they *not* meet, right? How they did meet was through a mutual friend—a horse trainer, of course, who thought the two might like to partner in owning a racehorse called Regal Justice. They met, fell in love, and were off to the races in more ways than one.

$\mathcal{T}$hey chose a place called Bonnet Island Estate, beautifully situated on the Jersey shore, overlooking the grassy marshes of the Forsythe Wildlife Refuge. About three years ago the new owner, Chris Vernon, converted an old hunting lodge on the property into an inn comprising twelve rooms. Aiming especially to accommodate weddings, Chris needed a chapel and created one from a great barn he found in Vermont and had transported and reassembled here, piece by piece. And though Brendan and Adele chose to marry in the Catholic Church, the barn and the pastoral landscape of Bonnet Island suited them well. For me, the creative challenge was ridding myself of the beachy idea, which they chose not to focus on in their wedding festivities, apart from the implicit appreciation of the setting it provided: a sparkling bay, a brilliant blue sky, and the shimmering, golden light that only a perfect autumn day can offer.

## Season:

Early Fall

## Situation:

An afternoon wedding of about 250 guests with an equestrian theme and lots of nostalgic details.

## Setting:

Pastoral and elegantly rustic. Chapel wedding, with reception at a bayside inn adjacent to a beautiful wildlife refuge. Receiving line and drinks in a refurbished barn, leading to cocktails and hors d'oeuvres on a veranda over-looking the bay.

## Ideas and Inspirations

| HORSES | RIDING | TACK | BRIDLES | SADDLES | RIDING RINGS | RACEHORSES | RACING SILKS |
|---|---|---|---|---|---|---|---|
| RIDING CLOTHES | EQUIPMENT | HORSESHOES | LUCK | BLACK-SMITHS | GRAND-PARENTS' CANDY SHOPS | APPLES | HORSES LOVE APPLES |
| EVERYTHING ABOUT FALL | BERRIES | APPLES AND PEARS | HARVEST | COUNTRY | BARN | RUSTIC | COUNTRY |

# The Elements

## HORSESHOE

This was a particularly nice Element because while it obviously relates to horses, it is also a symbol of good luck. Its wonderful, sculptural shape made it easy to incorporate throughout the papery and versatile in combination with other Elements. It also doesn't hurt that the horseshoes themselves are inexpensive. We bought aluminum ones online for about a dollar apiece.

## CANDY

Both the bride and the groom have a serious sweet tooth that they come by honestly, as candy features prominently in both their family histories. Though their respective grandparents are deceased, they both were confectioners by trade, and the bride's sister has an ice cream shop in nearby Lavallette, New Jersey, where we often met to discuss wedding plans. The use of candy became a sweet (ahem) tribute to beloved family members no longer with us, and a fun and delicious way to play on the couple's personality. They danced the first dance to Sarah McLachlan's "Ice Cream."

## BERRIES

If flowering branches represent spring, berries represent fall. There could not be a more quintessential expression of autumn to me than lush branches of berries. They are bold and dynamic in arrangements and easily adapted for decoration. They can be wrapped around banisters, twisted into wreaths and garlands, or are beautiful just by themselves. Bittersweet and pyracantha (firethorn) are two of my favorites. By the way, be sure to wear gloves when you're working with firethorn. They aren't kidding about the thorn part.

## ORCHARD FRUITS

I love autumn weddings because the season itself is about abundance, harvest, and reaping what we've sown. Fruits of the orchard are particularly apt here since the bride and groom both live on working farms. There are so many varieties of apples and pears available today. Crab apples also work well. And their range of colors from gold to chartreuse to scarlet makes them perfect for our purposes here. Horses like them, too.

## The Colors

CRIMSON

BURGUNDY

PUMPKIN

RAW SIENNA

## The Details

I thoroughly enjoy every wedding I am involved with, but this one was especially fun because of its theme and the number of design ideas and details it inspired, beginning with the invitation. First of all, I cannot say enough about Karen Bartolomei of Grapevine, in Boston, with whom I have worked on so many beautiful and successful papery projects. Here, instead of the family crest at the top of the invitation, we applied a medallion of leather embossed with a horseshoe. Then we wrapped the card in leather and laced it up, like you might a riding boot. The envelope was lined in a blond woody color, echoing the wood in the refurbished barn where the couple received guests after the ceremony.

*T*he wedding itself was nearby, in a small country church whose quiet simplicity allowed the flowers really to "sing." The bridal bouquet was especially luscious because of its beautiful speckled roses, a species called Hocus Pocus. We also incorporated crab apples, burgundy calla lilies—so dramatic—and saracinia, which is a conical-shaped flower in white with burgundy veins. Chocolate cosmos are special because they only come out at this time of year, and the orange ranunculus really make it pop. There is also a little red cloverlike flower called gomphrena. A new design application my design director, Kim Hirst, tried here was wrapping the stems in yarn in addition to ribbon. It is literally warm and fuzzy and therefore appropriate to the season. The gold pins securing the yarn are a touch of warmth and luster.

This bouquet was also special in another way: Adele planned to toss it at the reception, as is customary, and there was a perfect spot from a balcony overlooking the room. As it sailed through the air, it broke into six smaller bouquets, which delighted the children and spread the happy superstition about "who is next."

# *In a departure from tradition . . .*

## WEDDINGS INCORPORATE MANY BEAUTIFUL TRADITIONS, SOME SENTIMENTAL

*and some practical. Therefore I hesitate in many cases to depart from time-honored practices, simply because they are there for a reason. Doing "something different" for its own sake just isn't always appropriate in the context of a wedding because while, yes, it is all about you, it is also about family and friends and the joining together of two people who will live and work and possibly raise a family in the midst of their community. Granted, in our high-speed, far-flung modern lives our communities of family and friends are all over the place, but that should not diminish our respect or enthusiasm for the customs that have served us well for centuries. Having said that, however, it doesn't mean we have to be sticks-in-the-mud or immune to alternatives.*

*One long-held tradition that seems to be fading fast is the showering of rice over the couple as they leave their reception and depart for their honeymoon. Rice, as a symbol of fertility and abundance, represents good luck and the wish for children and prosperity. But today rice is considered a bit of a nuisance and environmentally incorrect (bad for the birds), so replacements are called for. Birdseed, flower petals, confetti, and even bubbles have all proved popular with modern brides. At my cousin's wedding all of the guests rang little bells as the couple exited the church. It was charming.*

*Another tradition that may have outlived its practicality is the timing of the petal/birdseed/confetti toss. Conventionally, at the reception after the cake is cut and the bouquet and garter are tossed, the couple change into their "going away" clothes and leave for the honeymoon. This exit is, or was, usually a mad dash for the car as guests barraged the couple with rice, birdseed, flower petals, whatever. Today's bridal couples, however, may often outlast some of their guests at the reception,*

*particularly the older set. The newlyweds understandably want to stay and party with their friends, while the older guests understandably may be ready to go home. For this reason nowadays we often have the petal toss after the ceremony, as the couple leaves the church. To be on the safe side, be sure to check first with the location to find out what is and is not allowed to be tossed in or outside their premises.*

*Of course, confetti and petals aren't the only thing tossed at weddings. One of the highlights of the reception is always the tossing of the bride's bouquet. All the single females gather together as the bride turns her back to them and throws the bouquet over her shoulder. As the superstition goes, whoever catches it will be the next to marry. Children invariably get a kick out of this as well—sometimes escaping a parent's grip to clamor for the bouquet themselves.*

*Because this is such a fun and exciting part of the evening and because there were so many children present, our bride Adele figured why not spread it around a bit? Instead of the traditional single bouquet, Adele's broke into six smaller bouquets as she pitched it over the balcony, to the surprise and delight of everyone. And since the children were leaving early, she moved this event up earlier in the evening especially to include them.*

*As the children were not staying for dinner, Adele also did not mind serving dessert first. The candy station is normally reserved for later in the evening, as an after-dinner treat, but we included it here in the cocktail hour. It was a thoughtful gesture on the bride's part, sweet in more ways than one. If departing from tradition makes an already good thing better, I am all for it.*

The flower girls' cones couldn't have been any cuter, if I do say so myself. The cones themselves are wrapped in fuzzy yarn and tied with rawhide laces. Bright red crab apples border and dangle from one, while tiny green pears adorn the other. The golden and red rose petals filling each reflect the bride's bouquet.

The key to the boutonniere was finishing it with rust-colored yarn and then wrapping it with crinkled copper wire. (Green floral tape be gone!) The vivid orange ranunculus, red gomphrena, and steel berry viburnum made for an unusual combination that definitely got itself noticed but didn't go overboard. We used the same gold pins for them as we did for the bride's bouquet.

Most appropriately, the wedding program's cover bore a photo of Regal Justice, the horse that brought Brendan and Adele together. Bearing Karen Bartolomei's inimitable stamp again, the vellum overleaf shrouded the image in a bit of softness and romance. On the first page was a story, in brief fairy tale form, about how the bride and groom met. This was a nice touch, particularly because it gave people a better understanding of what brought them together, their love for horses, and their love for each other as well. The bronze-colored ink on ivory paper was consistent throughout the papery and reflective of the overall color scheme, and of course we repeated the horseshoe emblem as a graphic element inside.

# The Wedding Program

## WEDDING PROGRAMS REALLY RUN THE GAMUT THESE DAYS. I FIND MORE

*and more couples wanting to deviate from the classic traditional program to something more personal and stylized. In Adele and Brendan's case we designed a program whose cover bore a picture of the very horse that was the reason for their meeting. Some couples fill in the usual schedule and lists with their own clever prose, while others find a place in the program to recall the memory of or pay tribute to loved ones no longer with us. While it is acceptable to expand the format of the wedding program and even to be a bit creative with its content, bear in mind that the program is about the ceremony. And the ceremony, religious or not, is the solemn part of the day and should be handled respectfully.*

On the grounds of Bonnet Island Estate is a large old barn that the owner salvaged in Vermont and had shipped piece by piece and reassembled in New Jersey. It is used both as a meeting place and as a chapel, and though the couple were married in a church, they did receive guests here after the ceremony before going on to cocktails on the adjacent porch, which overlooked the water. It was still a bit warm for a fire in that magnificent stone fireplace, but to play it up we illuminated it with tall cylindrical candles and votives.

For the enormous barn doors we created equally enormous wreaths—nearly as big as the doors themselves. Sturdy, woody grapevines formed the structure around which we wove bittersweet, pyracantha, viburnum berry, apples, pears, roses, and chrysanthemums. The chartreuse viburnum was a nice contrasting accent and complemented the red tones.

Inside the barn we wrapped columns in grapevine, again as a base, and then added pyracantha, bittersweet, viburnum, and fruit.

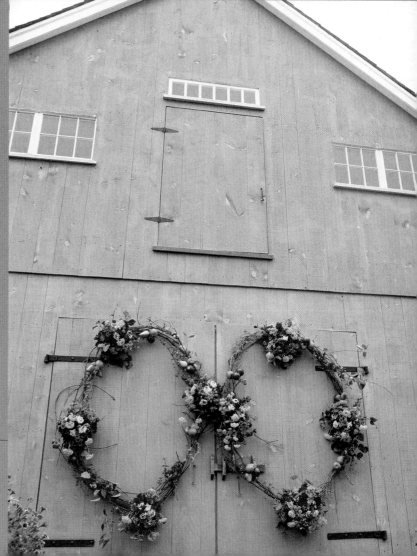

The ledges along the barn walls were lined in votive candles, which these days are made with different "burn times." I always buy the fifteen-hour ones. That way we can light them early and be done with it.

The seating card table actually wasn't one in this case. A set of old white barn doors were hinged together so they could free-stand, and the cards were hung from upholstery tacks, which are both substantial and decorative. The cards were banded with a horseshoe-embossed leather strip, repeating the motif of the invitation. Leather ties were knotted simply through grommets, all of which made a handsome, and unusual, presentation. Instead of numbering the tables, we gave them names of famous racehorses: Secretariat, Man O' War, Seabiscuit, and so on.

ishing to represent all of our Elements in the cocktail reception, we wrapped the table arrangements' rectangular vases in leather laces, yarn, or bailing twine and hot glued them with fruit. The votives were banded in suede ribbon stamped with crisscross or diamond motifs, to resemble patterns on a jockey's racing silks. We used saracinia again and steel berry viburnum.

The cocktail hour stretched to about an hour and a half because the bride had invited fifty or so of her young riding students to share in the celebration, though they would not be staying on for dinner. It is also part of the reason why we gave special emphasis to the candy station and why we placed it the cocktail area instead of the dinner area where it might usually go. It was a big hit with the children, of course, but it was also special as a tribute to family as well.

Inspiration for the table's design came from the stone fireplace and from the materials and finishes of the barn itself—the smooth texture of the rocks; the rustic walls and beams; the warm, rich glow of the polished floorboards. The range of beiges, creams, and browns reinforced our entire palette and lent itself easily to the decorative (and edible!) elements of the table.

A distressed old window made a series of frames for photos of the couple's grandparents presiding over their respective candy shops. Inserted into the remaining frames were brief descriptions and histories of the shops, and a menu of the evening's sweet offerings. The style and printing of the inserts were consistent with the invitations, program, and seating cards, so it was all of a piece.

Enhancing the vintage feel of our nostalgic details were old-fashioned glass canisters that fit neatly into the cubbies of what was once part of an old chicken coop. Because the couple loves horses, and horses love apples, a candied version of the favored fruit was a must. Fluted baking tins made pretty serving dishes. Chocolate-covered pretzels—while they lasted—were proffered in craft paper containers again applied with our horseshoe-stamped leather strip.

Candies were deliberately made or chosen for their size, shape, and color: caramels, chocolates, and buttercreams. Neon jellybeans and pink cupcakes just wouldn't have worked here. But equestrian-themed cookies made by the caterer were a perfect finishing touch.

# Let Them Eat Candy

## CANDY STATIONS ARE EXTREMELY POPULAR NOWADAYS, AND I ENJOY

doing them because they have such great creative potential. Like the seating card table, the candy station can be a destination unto itself. From little boxes or bags decorated with your special design Elements and colors to custom-made confections with couple's names or the bride's new initials, candy stations offer all sorts of possibilities for presentation. Adele's had a country feeling reflecting her reception's rural setting. At another wedding we sourced a wrought-iron garden stand to complement the gardenlike Midsummer's Night theme of the reception decor. At a wedding in Mexico, we created an entire station around the bright bold colors of the country and, of course, incorporated piñatas!

With Adele and Brendan, the opportunity was exceptional because not only did both sets of their grandparents own sweets shops and the couple had sweet tooths themselves, but their wedding festivities included about fifty children who were the couple's respective riding students. And I don't know about you, but when I was ten and faced with the choice between smoked salmon and a Tootsie Roll, I would probably have gone with the Tootsie Roll.

For the reception dinner, tables were dressed with two-tone silk dupioni in deep magenta and bronze, with hem-stitched napkins dyed magenta to match. The burgundy grosgrain ribbon tied loosely around the napkins trailed to the floor and fluttered when guests pulled out their chairs, which was nice. The long ribbons also gave a visual dimension to the oft-ignored side of the table, adding a little shimmer and texture.

Instead of being assigned numbers, the tables were named for famous racehorses. We did the research to come up with old black-and-white photos of each horse, which we spray-mounted on heavy cardboard and backed in caramel-colored leather. Each photo was propped against a cylinder candle and placed on the table, adding yet another nostalgic touch while also reinforcing our equestrian theme.

For the centerpieces, wide-mouthed pedestal vases accommodate lush, low, spreading arrangements that are just right for seventy-two-inch round dinner tables. Here we have dahlias, plumosa, bittersweet, Isle de France tulips, apples and pears, and four species of roses: Black Magic (red), Abracadabra (red with yellow flecks), Gypsy Curiosa (yellow with red tips), and Lemonade spray roses. Glass cylinders holding candles created more reflected light, which is something to keep in mind for evening weddings.

UNBRIDLED

As the number of guest rooms at the estate was relatively small—twelve in all—we felt we could afford to go a little overboard with the goodies. Nice-size willow baskets were affixed with horseshoes for good luck and filled with a bounty of fruit, flowers, and candy. Roses, gomphrena, and ranunculus are tied into posies. Mrs. Prindable's chocolate-covered apples are wrapped in cellophane and closed with our horseshoe-stamped leather. Bundles of fruit and boxes of sweets are prettily tied with rust-colored satin and wired chartreuse organza—all tasteful (and tasty!) reminders of a very special weekend.

# About Theme Weddings

**BRENDAN AND ADELE WERE SO ENTHUSIASTIC ABOUT CONTRIBUTING THEIR IDEAS**
to their big weekend. And they both had such a playful point of view that it was easy—and a joy—to become caught up in the spirit of the story we would tell.

Because I see every wedding as a story with a beginning, middle, and end, I believe all weddings have themes. Whether I consider it an "internal" theme as my own creative compass, or an "external" theme arrived at with the client, there is some kind of narrative thread for every event I do because it gives direction and perspective to the creative process. It is subtle when the tone of the wedding sets the theme, as with our classic St. Regis wedding on pages 102–118; and obvious when the theme sets the tone, as it most certainly did with Brendan and Adele.

But there's that word, theme, which can sort of make people cringe. There is a difference between amusing and delighting your guests with a series of inspired details . . . and beating them over the head with "Brand You." For example, an object like a horseshoe or a seashell can become an emblem engraved formally on papery, used decoratively in table arrangements, or repeated whimsically on gift baskets. Each reference to "theme"

is varied to suit the context so it can be re-experienced from a fresh perspective.

On a trip I took to Marrakech where I stayed at La Mamounia, I was struck by the fact that the curlicue "LM" logo was everywhere. It drove me bananas. But keep in mind that you are hosting a wedding, and that it is a religious ceremony (in most cases) and a social occasion, not a marketing opportunity.

The key to a successful theme is balance and variety, particularly for a destination wedding, where you have a captive audience for three or four days. In a way that mere flowers and linens cannot, Elements of a well-executed theme thread the weekend's events together both creatively and conceptually, while expressing who you are. There is more-over the significant, if subconscious, effect of bringing your guests together. You are giving them all the inside story, making them feel even more welcome and included. This is your gift to them.

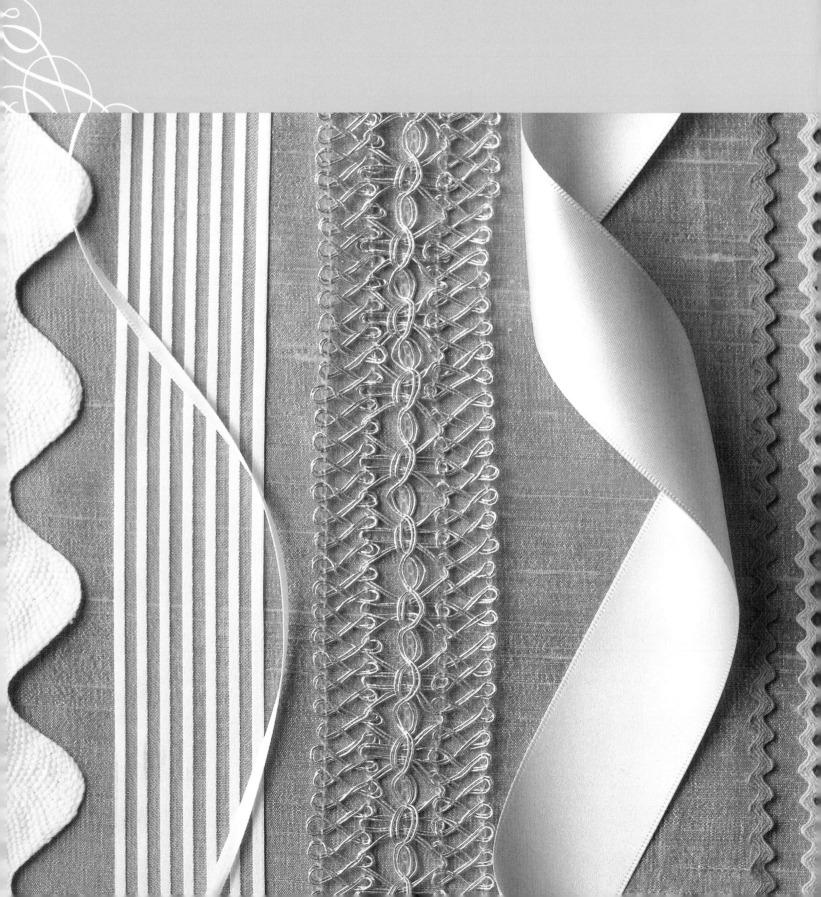

Heather Turben knew Matthew Schimenti was *the one* when, after regaling him via telephone with the details of a bad day, Matthew (in Connecticut) jumped in the car and headed toward Heather (in New York). "I'm on my way, and I'm taking you somewhere special." As she waited for him to drive in, she had plenty of time to imagine what fabulous and romantic spot she was about to be whisked off to. And though the destination certainly surprised her, it did not disappoint. Matthew took Heather to the Magnolia Bakery. He knew how much his sweetheart loved sweets in general and cupcakes in particular, and he had heard the famed Greenwich Village bakery's were the best in town. And as anybody who lives in New York knows, every Friday night finds a line around the block inching its way toward Magnolia's tiny counter. The sheer spontaneity of Matthew's act and the pure sweetness of it, Heather says, convinced her he was the guy for her. The rest was all, well, icing on the cupcake, shall we say?

*I* figured any girl who'd fall for a fellow over a cupcake must have a great sense of whimsy and fun, and I was right. But Heather is also quite sophisticated and chic, with an attractive feminine, almost girly quality that is old-fashioned and modern at the same time. All those characteristics gave us a lot to work with in terms of details, and for a number of reasons this was a wedding all about the details.

Theirs was not a long engagement, and by the time I came into the picture the location, the Delamar Hotel in Greenwich, Connecticut, was already chosen by Heather and wedding planner Liz Securro. We quickly determined the color palette—Connecticut preppy pink and green—and decided to play off the hotel's Old World architectural elements, particularly the scrolls and flourishes of its decorative ironwork.

$\mathcal{T}$he reception began with cocktails on the veranda overlooking a stormy, rainy harbor (more on this later), but the wedding party was undeterred and the subdued lighting and feeling of huddling up made it all the more romantic. Dinner, fortunately, was inside.

## Season:

Early Winter

## Setting:

The ceremony takes place in a pretty old stone church in town; the reception in a waterfront hotel in New England.

## Situation:

A seven P.M. wedding with two hundred guests. The church is non-denominational, as the bride is Lutheran and the groom Catholic. Hotel where reception held also lodged out-of-town guests. Formal dinner in the hotel ballroom following cocktails on the covered porch.

## Ideas and Inspirations

| | | | | | |
|---|---|---|---|---|---|
| RIBBON | | SILVER | SPECIALTY COCKTAILS | | METALLIC | |
| | CLASSIC | | CANDLELIGHT | | TRADITIONAL | CUPCAKES |
| ICING | | THE COLORS OF ICING | | ICING SWIRLS | | SWIRLY DESIGNS |
| | CURLICUES | | SWEETS | | PREPPY | PINK |
| OLD WORLD | | FLIRTY | | EUROPEAN | | TEXTURE |
| | NORWEGIAN | | CONNECTICUT | | WHIMSY | GREEN |

## SILVER LEAF

With its cool luster and connotations of pedigree and propriety, the Element of silver, whether in the form of silver leaf, silver paint, or silver itself lends a bit of aesthetic gravitas to a decorative scheme otherwise very much in touch with its playful side. A contemporary gleam of metal here and there also gave our more traditional Elements a fresh, modern edge.

## CURLICUES

I love the scrolls and motifs of the Delamar Hotel's decorative ironwork and architecture, and curling motifs are a fun way to embellish so many decorative Elements. Bold and curvaceous, or feathery and soft, a curlicue is the decorative equivalent of a wink—flirtatious and a little sassy.

## RIBBON

I grew up in Princeton, New Jersey, in the seventies during the height of the preppy craze. My sister and I must have had every Fair Isle sweater and ribbon belt known to man and Talbots. Ribbon is the quintessential preppy element, so why not embrace it? Inexpensive and easy to incorporate in a myriad of details, ribbon can be tied into everything from papery to flowers to favors. Ribbons and bows make the most mundane package into a present, and I find that analogy works on many levels from a decorative perspective. Ribbons signify gifts, whether literal or figurative, and somehow instill a sense of joyful anticipation.

## The Colors

SILVER

BUBBLEGUM PINK

MINT GREEN

WHITE

## The Details

*J*ust because we had a major preppy thing going on here didn't mean our designs had to be stuck in the 1970s. The invitation combines both modern and preppy design Elements, with white stock mounted on a metallic silver card. The bride's and groom's names are printed in hot pink and the remaining type is in silver. The piece is delicately wound with a single silver wire threaded with pink faceted beads. The sage green envelope is lined with pink polka dot paper and pink tissue.

Following the ceremony, guests proceeded to the hotel for the reception. Large standing arrangements at the drive-up entrance to the hotel signified immediately to guests that they had arrived at the wedding. Often at hotels I am unable to extend the wedding décor to the hotel street entrance. But at the Delamar Hotel it was possible. A pair of grand arrangements flanking the door under the porte-cochere signalled the festivities were underway within.

THE PLEASURE OF
YOUR COMPANY IS REQUESTED
AT THE MARRIAGE OF

HEATHER
TURBEN

TO

MATTHEW
SCHIMENTI

SATURDAY, THE FIFTEENTH OF OCTOBER
TWO THOUSAND AND FIVE
AT HALF AFTER FIVE IN THE EVENING
THE DELAMAR HOTEL
GREENWICH, CONNECTICUT

*T*ussie-mussies of pink and white ranunculus with white delphiniums and tulips are finished with double-faced pale pink satin fastened with pink pins and trailing metallic silver ribbon and rickrack. The juxtaposition of the shiny, modernish ribbon and the sort of lowly, homespun rickrack has a certain charm. I also especially like using the buds of a flower, in this case the ranunculus, because they add movement and dimension.

In the spirit of giving traditional details a modern edge, we chose a textured, silver metallic paper for the petal toss cone itself and managed to incorporate all our Elements in this one piece. A wired, silver metallic ribbon is easily coiled into curlicues, while the more traditional satin ribbon trails softly alongside. The cones were filled with pink delphiniums, which are more floaty and frilly than the usual rose petals—a small flourish that dresses up this detail appropriately for a dressed-up evening occasion.

# *Personal Flowers*

## THROUGHOUT HISTORY FLOWERS HAVE OCCUPIED A PLACE IN LIFE'S RITES

*of passage. The brides of ancient Greece wore wreaths of flowers in their hair, and the Victorians contrived an entire language of flowers. The symbology of flowers is both powerful and enduring, as is their evocative sensory experience.*

*Flowers are my first love when it comes to design, and I still approach each arrangement with a sense of wonder and delight. One of the best things about making bouquets today is that with sophisticated growing techniques and overnight delivery services from almost everywhere, some of my favorite flowers have become practically seasonless. Viburnums in September! Lilacs in October! It's great. But if you live in a place where the selections are limited, do not despair. Bouquets and boutonnieres are about silhouette, texture, and color, and a good designer can achieve good results with whatever is at hand.*

*I also find that brides today are creative and outspoken when it comes to their bouquets. They see the bouquet not only as an important complement to the dress but also as a distinct stylistic statement.*

*When it comes to the bridesmaids' flowers, they should be distinct from the bride's, of course, but not look like the "poor relations." I love tussie-mussies, or nosegays, for their diminutive shape and size. When you have a large bridal party, smaller flowers are better. A lot of big, fluffy, leafy arrangements can be overwhelming, whereas smaller bouquets create a better visual balance, particularly in photographs.*

*According to tradition, the groom's boutonniere should be handpicked from the bride's bouquet. And as with the bride's and bridesmaids' bouquets, the groomsmen's boutonnieres should be distinguishable from the groom's, all the more important since they are all usually dressed alike.*

*My bouquets do not begin and end with flowers, however. Beautiful ribbons and decorative pins, "findings" used in sewing such as buttons and gimp, various trimmings and rickrack, silk brocade, embroidery appliqués, even broaches and other bits of jewelry—all are possibilities for embellishing personal flowers. If you are a person who haunts flea markets and garage sales, as I am, keep your eyes peeled for small treasures that might transform your bouquet into yet another expression of your creative personality.*

The groom's boutonniere was comprised of a single white delphinium and one ranunculus bud, with the flourish of a silver coil—a striking contrast against the black of the groom's tuxedo lapel. The groomsmen's boutonnieres were the same construction as the groom's, but in pale pink and minus the extra curlicue.

White tulips, lilacs, ranunculus, lady's slippers, and Eucharist lilies wrapped with silver coils and white ribbon make up the bride's bouquet. A jewel-like cuff, almost like a bracelet, is formed with silver brocade appliquéd with silver curlicues and white pearl pins.

Heather was a beautiful bride—she was the picture of anticipation and radiance. All the rain in the world could not dampen her spirits. Here she excitedly waits for her car before going to the church.

# Specialty Cocktails

## SPECIALTY DRINKS ARE SUCH A NICE TOUCH FOR ANY PARTY, AND A PRACTICAL

one, too, as they can be prepared in advance and so help prevent that initial bottleneck at the bar. Whether it's a champagne cocktail, a Bellini, or even a margarita if it suits the occasion—or whether you whip up your own concoction as Heather and Matthew did—it's another way to convey to your guests the care and consideration you've taken to entertain and amuse them. And of course tasty libations, presented in an artistic and colorful way are yet another creative outlet to savor. Interesting trays, glasses, and garnishes offer many design possibilities. From a practical standpoint, having a waiter greet guests at the door with a tray of prepared cocktails,

along with sparkling water and perhaps champagne, has a lovely way of preventing a bottleneck at the bar. (Nothing is worse than having to wait for a drink. . . .) Your signature cocktail might be served at one or more of the events during your wedding weekend; it need not be specifically reserved for the reception. Another nice touch is to pair the cocktail with the food being served. Bellinis with Italian fare, for example; or a sake-based drink with Asian food. That way the drinks complement the cuisine and make for a more enjoyable gastronomic statement.

*G*reen metallic monograms give the white cocktail napkins a little zip, and what's more preppy than a monogram? As for the drinks themselves, all I knew was that they had to be pink and green, and I give Paul Toro, L'Escale's bartender and mixologist, full credit for creating these perfectly hued potions. L'Escale is the Delamar's restaurant connected to the hotel ballroom where the wedding and reception were held. The Pretty in Pink is—you guessed it—pink, and the Pauladori is green. If you're going to invent a cocktail, might as well name it after yourself, right? At least he is nice enough to give us the recipes. We also specially selected glassware with our Elements' metallic touches.

## PRETTY IN PINK

2 ounces Absolut vodka

1 ounce Chambord

$^1/_2$ ounce simple syrup

1 ounce fresh lime juice

1 ounce fresh lemon juice

Splash of 7Up

Ice

Lime wedge and maraschino cherry,
for garnish

Mix all ingredients in a shaker and serve in a Collins or highball glass, and garnish with lime wedge and cherry.

## PAULADORI

1 $^1/_2$ ounces Midori

2 $^1/_2$ ounces Citadel Raspberry Vodka

$^1/_4$ ounce fresh lime juice

2 ounces pineapple juice

1 ounce 7Up

Ice

Lemon or lime twist, for garnish

Mix all ingredients in a shaker and serve in a chilled martini glass with a lemon or lime twist.

Because of its placement just outside the ballroom where dinner was served—and therefore technically in the hotel lobby—the seating card table was in full and frequent view throughout the evening. Not only was it a design element, it was a sort of semi-destination—a transitional point that gave decorative continuity to the evening. It also served as a subtle, if beautiful, signal to other hotel patrons that a special event was under way and thereby possibly saving them the embarrassment of bounding into the restaurant to ask for a table for two.

This large—nearly four feet high—and shapely tree is sprayed with silver paint to look as if dusted with silver leaf. It is "planted" on the table, secured to a spike with plastic cable ties on a sturdy metal plate. White phalaenopsis orchids in florists' vials are wired to the branches, and votive candles in clear glass containers are hung with silver wire. Covering the base are river rocks, chosen for their smooth roundness as well as their silver-gray color. Larger stones around the base segue to smaller stones at the periphery, which serve as perfect holders for the seating cards, in white with silver calligraphy.

The cocktail table arrangements were flirtatious and chic. Silver leaf cylinders were filled with hot-pink spray roses, and delicate silver wire was threaded throughout the blooms.

White ceramic cachepots filled with hot-pink spray roses and pink gomphrena are suspended by silver scrolls and flourishes and hung in clusters of three. Each cluster of arrangements—about twenty in all—was accompanied by five or so hanging votives, for a very pretty overall effect on the veranda where cocktails were held. And unlike standard table arrangements, these are visible above the guests' heads.

While we used the restaurant's tablecloths and china for dinner, we did a few things on the tables to liven them up a little, like renting bright green wineglasses and dyeing napkins to match. Pink cymbidiums at each place setting keep the color scheme going, and the centerpieces take the same white vases from the porch, continuing the same scroll and tassel motif—whimsical and fun. Flowers are pink spray roses, pink and white stock, and gomphrena.

There was a commanding fireplace right in the center of the dining room. Following the ceremony the couple wanted to take photographs there, so we pulled out the stops and placed as much pillar candlelight as the maitre d' would allow. Very chic and Old World.

*Let* them eat cupcakes! It was Matthew's spiriting his true love off to the storied Magnolia Bakery that convinced her he was the one, so cupcakes were the perfect guest take-aways. Ours are iced in pink and green, naturally, and from nowhere other than Magnolia itself. They have to have sprinkles, of course, and the little boxes and scalloped labels complete their pretty presentation.

# *Weather Happens*

**YES, RAIN, SNOW, ICE, WIND, EXCRUCIATING HEAT, AND BONE-CHILLING COLD** *are very real factors in planning any party, and one of the universe's most effective reminders that we are not always completely in charge. For your wedding day, a contingency plan ensures a smooth day. The most important thing, though, is to take it all in stride. So-called gloomy weather is only gloomy if you let it be. As a matter of fact, I find rain makes for very moody photos and creates a very cozy atmosphere. Everyone participating exudes a "we're all in this together" feeling that makes for great camaraderie and a most convivial group. Besides, rain at a wedding is said to be good luck, and a good storm is exciting!*

The bride is Scandinavian by heritage and the grand-daughter of an excellent baker. We arranged for the hotel's pastry chef to prepare some of her grandmother's most beloved cookie recipes and offered them on the sweets table, which also included the bride's favorite candies: Good & Plenty, Jelly Belly, and Red Hots. The guests ate them up! For an extra-special touch we had the cookie recipes printed on cards and displayed in silver frames.

As an aside, such special requests of hotel and catering staff are not only nice personal touches from the hosts but are implicit compliments to the chef or cook as well. It demonstrates your confidence in them and involves them more intimately in the enthusiasm and spirit of the occasion, which gives them something to be proud of. This is the sort of sharing of goodwill that benefits all parties.

*T*he bridesmaids' gifts made such a splash. We covered hatboxes with green-and-white-striped silk dupioni, edged with silver cord and tied with double-faced silver satin. Inside under a sprinkling of delphinium blossoms were cotton BedHead pajamas (the best!), a terrycloth wrap, and the hotel's own Bulgari amenities, conveniently green and white. Tucked into each was a note, telling each individual bridesmaid why the bride was especially glad she had come and what their friendship meant to her. As our bride in this case was not fond of her own handwriting, she had a calligrapher inscribe the cards, but the thoughtfulness of her very personal gesture was not diminished in the least.

*N*o doubt these notes are tucked safely away with every one of these bridesmaids' most cherished keepsakes, held dear as their memories of this happy day and their friendship with this lovely bride—sweet as a cupcake herself.

# Candlelight and Mirrors

As much as I love working closely with a bride and groom, it is not always possible. Their careers may be so demanding that they are unable to devote the time required by the myriad of details that go into designing a wedding. Or they may live so far from the wedding site that their hands-on participation is simply impractical. True on both counts in this case, but luckily the bride's parents, Kathi and Alan Glist, were all too happy to put on the show themselves. In fact I dealt almost exclusively with the parents to stage this glitzy, ritzy wedding. I use the words "show" and "stage" deliberately, as the parents are Broadway producers. And what is showier than a big splash at The Breakers, Palm Beach's famously grand hotel, smack in the middle of high season.

The Glists had booked The Breakers almost as soon as their daughter, Taryn, and her fiancé, Eduardo Rioseco, announced their engagement. And as the business of theater production is not exactly known to be low risk, it was not surprising that the Glists had not much intention of playing it safe from a design standpoint, either. And while they definitely wanted a design that was somewhat "outside the box," the bride did not want a feeling of being "branded" or overly themed. Nor did they want any sort of creampuff "bridey" look. Creampuffs, no; but clouds, yes. The father described to me how he wanted to achieve a cloudlike feeling in the room, like that feeling when you are in a plane and just above the clouds—light, airy, atmospheric, and ethereal. He wanted the guests to feel transported to another time and place, as they might well experience watching one of his theatrical productions. With them it was all about creating a sophisticated and stylized environment.

## Season:

Winter

## Setting:

The Breakers hotel in Palm Beach, with ceremony in the Circle Dining Room and dinner-dance in the Venetian Ballroom.

## Situation:

A formal and traditional Jewish ceremony followed by dinner and dancing, 275 guests. Because the couple lives on the West Coast, almost all wedding arrangements are to be made by her parents, who divide their time between Manhattan and Palm Beach.

## Ideas and Inspirations

| CLOUDLIKE | LIGHT | AIRY | ETHEREAL | ATMOSPHERIC | FLOATING | WISPY | OTHER-WORLDLY |
|---|---|---|---|---|---|---|---|
| ENVIRONMENTAL | THEATRICAL | DRAMATIC | STAGED | LOVES CANDLELIGHT | CANDELABRA | FLAME | ROMANTIC |
| WARM | WINTER | SNOW | WHITE | SILVER | MIRROR | REFLECTIVE | WHITE |
| FEATHERS | CRYSTALS | STYLIZED | SOPHISTICATED | SLEEK | METALLIC | MODERN | GLAMOUR |

# The Elements

## CRYSTALS

Regardless of the setting, crystals are a great wintertime element. Icy, cool, and sparkling, crystals can be elegant and subtle or they can bring on the bling.

## CANDLELIGHT

Candlelight is a very effective way to create warmth, with the bonus that as a form of light it is always flattering. And, of course, it is incredibly romantic. Regardless of your design direction, whether highly traditional or super-modern, candlelight works. It is one of the most versatile wedding design Elements there is.

## MIRROR SHARDS

Cool and edgy, mirror shards have a modern feel. They represent ice and are highly reflective of candlelight. They are also highly adaptive. Mirrors can be used by themselves, of course, as we did at dinner with the chargers, or applied to other surfaces in a sparkly, glinting mosaic.

## PAPER

I love paper, always have. I collect it, and I have a huge box of notecards I refer to from time to time. There are so many interesting and beautiful textured papers on the market today. It seemed an obvious element to transform glass cylinders holding the candles, but we carried it much further than that.

## ORCHIDS

We chose phalaenopsis orchids because they are clean, delicate, and dramatic, with a structural quality that makes them striking used alone or in masses. Also, of all the orchids they are the softest in shape—round and pretty.

## WHITE FEATHERS

Graceful, soft, and flirty. We were not working with a lot of flowers (except orchids) in this design. I find that other natural elements in lieu of flowers lend a wonderful texture and lushness to arrangements. Feathers are also fun, playful, and happy.

# The Colors

SILVER ●     GOLD ●     PEARL WHITE ○

# The Details

**A** glamorous invitation heralds a glamorous party. Ours is a gold dupioni-silk-covered board edged in ribbon and punctuated with an adhesive-backed crystal—quite a production. For safe mailing the invitation required a specially designed folder called a pocket cover, which is then put in an envelope to mail. Be aware that unusually shaped or elaborate invitations such as these probably will require extra postage. I once worked with a bride who ordered a traditional Tiffany's invitation and expected nothing out of the ordinary when it came to mailing them—indeed it hadn't even crossed her or her mother's mind. After hand-addressing and stamping all 800 or so, she took them to her small-town post office only to be told another ten cents was required for each one. Ack! The moral of that story is to check with the post office and have the invitation weighed first, so you know exactly what you are getting into.

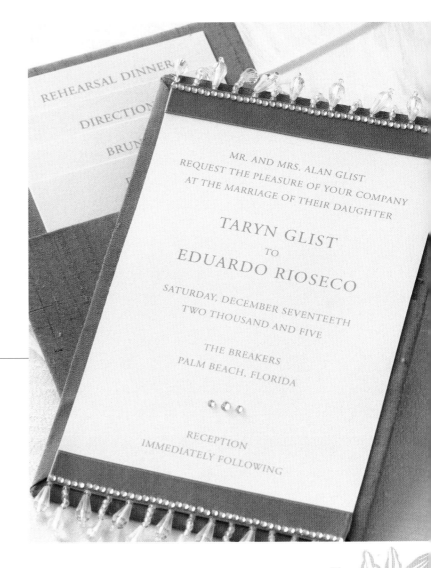

REHEARSAL DINNER

DIRECTION

BRUN

MR. AND MRS. ALAN GLIST
REQUEST THE PLEASURE OF YOUR COMPANY
AT THE MARRIAGE OF THEIR DAUGHTER

TARYN GLIST
TO
EDUARDO RIOSECO

SATURDAY, DECEMBER SEVENTEETH
TWO THOUSAND AND FIVE

THE BREAKERS
PALM BEACH, FLORIDA

RECEPTION
IMMEDIATELY FOLLOWING

In keeping with our color scheme, the bridal flowers were all white, a bouquet of Vendela and Majolica spray roses with large diamond-shaped crystals hand-wired throughout. A wrapping of white satin and a cuff of feathers and dendrobium orchids on ribbon tendrils finished it, giving it movement and an elegant finish.

The boutonnieres were fashioned from roses, crystals, feathers, and gold trimmings, with gold wire securing the ribbon-wrapped stems.

# The Ceremony

## AT ONCE JOYFUL AND SOLEMN, A WEDDING CEREMONY IS ABOVE ALL A

*sacred rite signifying a sacred union. If at the outset of your planning process you are nonchalant about your ceremony, I will tell you that its importance tends to sneak up on you. As it should; the ceremony is important. As a ritual, the ceremony is the only part of the wedding weekend where you, together with your family and friends, are removed from the outside world both literally and figuratively. However momentarily, the language, symbols, and traditions of the ceremony take you out of your everyday world and into a realm of spirit and contemplation. You and your groom have an opportunity in this space to slow down and to consider a wedding ceremony that reflects who you are and acknowledges how you arrived at where you are at that moment. Not every bride needs to walk down a seventy-five-foot aisle or ride up on a white horse, but there are ways to personalize your ceremony that are emotionally meaningful and everlastingly gratifying.*

*The design and content of the ceremony is a function of many factors, of which religious affiliation is only the beginning. We have couples for whom the religious aspect of the ceremony is paramount, and we have couples who want just to get it over with so they can get to the party. There are interfaith couples who wish to respect the religious practices of both their families, and other couples who incorporate customs from their national cultures or ethnic backgrounds. Still others create their own rite to reflect some aspect of their personal story.*

*Following an old Mexican tradition, one couple I know had a table at the altar to which members of the congregation were invited to bring objects symbolizing happiness and good luck—an ear of corn, a family photo, a set of rosary beads. Another bride and groom coincidentally were each in the habit of collecting sand from places they visited. At their wedding they poured their respective sand collections into one vessel, symbolizing the joining of their two lives. And in one of our chapters an African-American couple "jumps the broom" after saying their vows, symbolic of sweeping away the past and whatever troubles there might have been. You may want to have a friend read a favorite poem or a passage of scripture, or you may just go strictly by the book, and that is okay, too.*

*Otherwise I think it is best to keep these personalized features of ceremony fairly low key and to avoid anything that might appear gimmicky or schmaltzy. You don't want to look back and wonder what you were thinking. You do want to remember your ceremony as the sincere declaration of commitment that it is.*

The Breakers' ornately painted and gilded Circle Dining Room was the setting for the ceremony. When a space is heavily decorated such as this one, I tend to focus more on lighting and layout of the space itself—placement of chairs and so forth—and less or not at all on floral or architectural embellishment. We emphasized the color gold because there is so much of it already there, and gold is a warm, luxe color for winter. Also leaving the room décor to speak for itself allowed us to play up the chuppah and really make it the center of the room's attention, as it should be.

In accordance with the family's desire to have the ceremony reflect a sense of community, the chuppah was placed on an elevated round platform at the center of concentric circles of seating, which allowed family and friends literally to "gather 'round," with no one sitting too far back. It was an arrangement also perfectly suited to the room's circular shape.

The chuppah itself was a real showstopper, a gracefully constructed canopy of weeping willow branches. Stripped of its leaves, the willow bark has a golden hue that complemented our color scheme. Then we hand-wired dendrobium orchids and cymbidium orchids in clusters among the branches. Dramatic lighting from above and below gave the setting a theatrical flair, appropriate considering the hosts' provenance. And as a lovely, flickering, final detail, votive candles in clear glass containers were hung among the willows and orchids.

The wedding programs kept the glitz factor going, enfolded in metallic gold paper with crystal-studded ribbon spines. The bride's new monogram adorned the cover.

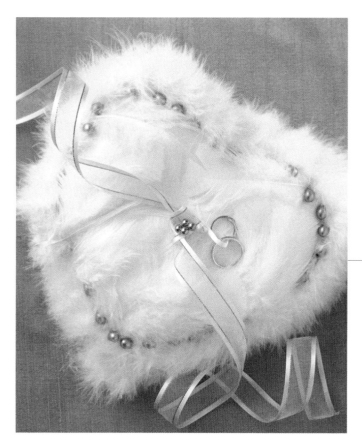

Our ring bearer's pillow was another little bit of showbiz flash: a heart-shaped cushion with a marabou feather cuff and gold, beaded trim.

If your guests must traverse a room or series of rooms to get from one part of the evening to another, it is important to make it as easy and attractive for them as possible. You don't want them all dressed up and ambling through some vast empty space. A little feng shui can go a long and sensible way. In this case, creating a passageway would make the space more coherent and keep the crowd and their energy from scattering. From a design perspective, there is also an opportunity here to make an atmospheric transition and build a sense of anticipation for what is to come. Our romantic *allée* of towering fourteen-foot trees constructed from willow branches and held together with heavy-duty industrial plastic cable ties did just that. Alternating with the trees were panels of decorative ironwork, arched metal screens that followed the arches of the room's windows and were hung with candlelight. Lit from above with spots and chandeliers and from below with candles in glass cylinders (hey, like footlights!), the aisle appeared to glow from the light reflected on the polished marble floor.

The curly willow branches were strung with hanging candlelight and entwined with dendrobium orchids, and the effect, as expressly desired, was truly ethereal and otherworldly. It was like a forest at night bathed in starlight and shadow.

The guest book was placed in the garden cocktail area to be signed before guests went into the Venetian Ballroom for dinner and dancing. With its mirror-encrusted cover and marabou spine, the book was a small work of art and a good way to reinforce our design Elements by keeping the guests in a certain visual train of thought.

$\mathcal{T}$he seating card table provided another dramatic focal point. A long window box encrusted in a mosaic of mirror shards holds a profuse planting of curly willow painted winter-white. A colony of feather butterflies nestled among the branches that were sprinkled with crystals, all sparkling in the light of hanging votives. The seating cards themselves were silver-lined white paper affixed with silver numerals and feathers, and studded with beautiful little silver-and-crystal flowers.

The dinner tables alternated between round and square, each seating from ten to fourteen guests. The shape of the table was complemented by its respective centerpiece design. Directives from the client steered me away from the classic floral centerpiece toward something less conventional. I saw a perfect opportunity there to echo our white willow designs, which we did for the round tables. Containers completely covered in white feathers held the gangly, curly branches with clusters of orchids (phalaenopsis this time) and votives.

Dinner was held in the hotel's Venetian Ballroom, which I approached as a blank canvas. To create our ethereal, cloudlike environment so stunningly set up by the walk through the willows, we began by softening the space overall with custom-made floor-to-ceiling sheer drapes. The room's enormous crystal chandeliers were lowered, enhancing the intimacy and scale of the setting. But the real magic was created by a grid of lightweight metal cable we were able to make using the room's various rigging points. (The Breakers' ballroom is particularly good for this because it has a lot of rigging points, which might be something you want to think or inquire about in your own reception space.) With the nearly invisible grid in place, we used fishing line to suspend candles in inverted bell-shaped vases at various heights throughout the room, to simulate starlight. Between the candlelight, the chandeliers, and the special ambient lighting, the sheer curtaining shimmered and gently billowed as if blown by an ocean breeze.

# Do the Light Thing

## LIGHTING SIMPLY MAKES ALL THE DIFFERENCE IN THE WORLD.

*It is the thing that absolutely makes a design come to life. Granted, not every bride has the budget to afford elaborate lighting, but it doesn't have to be elaborate or expensive to be effective. A simple up-light on your ceremony area not only draws attention to you but just as importantly draws it away from what you want to disappear. Lighting can hide a world of faults and right a world of decorating wrongs. (Fortunately at The Breakers we were not correcting but enhancing.)*

*Be mindful, however, that most public ceremony and reception venues are subject to fire codes and are rightfully careful about complying with them. These apply to electric light and to candlelight as well. With this wedding in particular, where candlelight was one of our Elements, the code*

*had to be complied with as part of our design. Specifically, regulations do not allow open, exposed flame. A flame must be enclosed in glass or below the surface level of its container. Our use here of lacy and decorative papers to wrap the glass cylinders was one very effective way to play by the rules. Suspending votives at various heights throughout the room, safely inside their little glass urns, was another.*

*I will caution you, though, from the logistics side of the clipboard: Elaborate lighting plans require time and manpower. For tent weddings time is plentiful as the tent is usually erected several days in advance, but hotels are different. Quite often hotel events and reception rooms are booked back-to-back.*

This showstopping menu card was both beautiful and playful. Another of my favorite design treatments is to print in the "graffiti" font and to use several different type sizes. For this design Grapevine Weddings used a double-thickness white card stock with metallic silver engraving. As the finishing touch faceted crystal fringe was hand-applied at top and bottom. Its placement was delicate on the organdy dinner napkins, which I loved for their sheer sexiness.

# Menu Cards

## AS YOU HAVE SURMISED BY NOW, I LOVE DETAIL AND PAPERY IN PARTICULAR.

*I think individual menus are a superb touch, especially if you have painstakingly chosen the meal and want to call attention to the food. Menus can also serve double duty by acting as a placecard with the individual guest's name written at the top of the menu. This also reduces the clutter on the table.*

*An opportunity to reinforce your design Elements, menu cards can be any texture or color, and I love playing with their shapes by die-cutting anything from leaves to circles. Embellished with fringe, tassels, crystals, flowers, hand painting, appliqués, or stickers, the menu can adopt a formal or casual look and project a serious or playful tone. As a decorative accessory to your table, the menu card is a definite asset, and when the party's over it becomes a lovely keepsake.*

The square tables had a more contained arrangement of lacy, paper-wrapped cylinder candleholders of varying heights arranged among clear square glass vases, one at each place, holding phalaenopsis. Some of the vases were dusted with feathers; some studded with crystals; some wound with snowy angora yarn; and some woven with white satin ribbon. This entire display was set on a twenty-inch round mirror.

All tables wore white cloths beneath sheer overlays sewn with white tassels from the edge of the table to the floor. (The theatrical influence here put me in touch with my inner costume mistress.) The white bamboo ballroom chairs benefited from the same treatment, with sheer slipcovers and tassels shimmying down the back and sides. Mirrored chargers at each place, square for the square tables and round for the round, brought together all the Elements to each table, for a look that was modern, jazzy, and sexy—and definitely outside the "bridey" box.

And finally the cake was a masterful effort by Ron Ben-Israel in New York. For Ron and his team design direction was easy. We supplied him with this great mosaic mirrored platform we found in the flower market, and these remarkable brainy bakers literally interpreted our Elements. The cake and its base together incorporate candlelight, mirror shards, orchids, crystals, feathers, and paper.

To sashay the night away, guests were gifted with white feather boas to bring out the diva in all of them. If weddings had curtain calls, this one would bring the house down—a glamorous, glittering performance worthy of a standing ovation.

# On Grand Hotels

**I'D LIKE TO SAY A PARTING WORD ABOUT THE CODDLING AND CONVENIENCE**
*of a grand hotel wedding and the luxurious amenities of spending the first night there. A real knows-what-it's-doing place like The Breakers can provide the quintessential romantic experience. Apart from its fabulous bridal suite and unsurpassed ocean views, newlyweds can order up a dollop of caviar and a sampling of sweets, all set on a silver tray at bedside with champagne for two. Cheers, you two!*

Kimberly Steward and Jamil Blackwell have been sweethearts since high school. Theirs is a story of patience and true love. Although Kimberly was the one to contact me about her wedding, once I met her parents I understood immediately how she came by her extraordinary qualities of enthusiasm, sincerity, and warmth. Even a stranger could see that Kimberly's parents are as in love today as the first night they met at a party so many years ago. Their relationship is built on trust and respect and Kim has taken those lessons into the world and found her soul mate. Over the entire twelve months of working together, there was never a cross word nor a tense moment. It is as though their love for one another envelops and cushions them, and what love doesn't fix, their ready laughter diffuses. Kimberly the bride knew exactly what she wanted from day one: a grand affair that would take St. Louis by storm. She loves flowers and vibrant colors, and her attention to detail was unflagging. She was a wonderful creative partner and I have no doubt that in the years to come she will approach any task at hand with her characteristic zeal and can-do attitude. Jamil was a supportive partner and a good sport. It isn't easy for a guy to take in all this girly stuff with the grace and poise he demonstrated. He was a delight, registering an opinion when necessary and knowing always just when a little levity was called for.

I don't usually comment on a couple's or family's faith or religious inclinations except as they relate to the conception of the wedding design, but in this instance I would be remiss to omit it. In working with the Stewards and Jamil, I came to understand that the source and strength of their bond and their deep affection for one another is their faith. Devotedly religious, Kimberly and her family possess an inner strength and confidence that was as encouraging for me in my work with them as it was inspiring.

*Setting:*

St. Louis, ceremony at Salem United Methodist Church followed by reception and dinner at Bellerive Country Club.

*Situation:*

A formal evening wedding and seated dinner for 325. Music to feature prominently, from gospel to jazz, to Motown.

*Ideas and Inspirations*

| PINK | GOLD | ORCHIDS | VINES | FLOWERS | CRYSTALS | GRAPEVINE | LUSH |
|---|---|---|---|---|---|---|---|
| EXTRAVAGANT | GRAND | BIG SPLASH | MAXIMUM IMPACT | HOT PINK | LIGHT PINK | FAMILY | FAITH |
| CHURCH | FOOD | SOUL MATES | SOUL FOOD | MUSIC | FRIENDS | PINK | DID I MENTION PINK? |

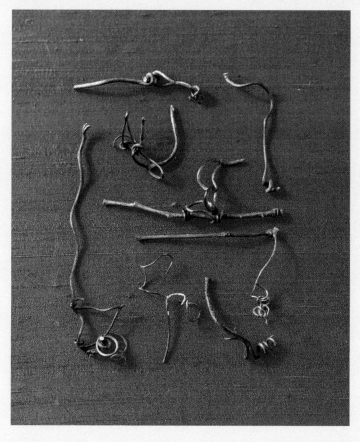

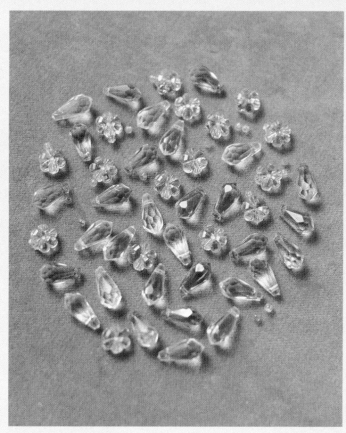

## PINK FLOWERS

This bride, more than any other bride featured in this book, could not have enough flowers. It was the most important Element to her (aside from pink). Did I mention pink?

## THE COLOR PINK

We chose pink as an Element because it is Miss Kim's favorite color. Lucky for us Mother Nature obliges with many, many choices in flowers. The range of pinks and the types of flowers in the pink family are almost endless.

## GRAPEVINE

Grapevine has wonderful movement and it represents the bare branches of winter. We also chose grapevine because in a completely organic way, it mimics the scrolls of the design carried throughout Kim and Jamil's papery.

## PINK CRYSTALS

The bride loves things that sparkle—just like her personality. From the candles to the cocktail vases, we wanted to give everything a glittery glow.

## The Colors

GOLD     ●        HOT PINK     ●

CREAM     ○        LIGHT PINK     ●

## The Details

From a design standpoint, the save-the-date card might also be thought of as the set-the-tone card, planting the seeds as it does for some of the most important elements of Kim and Jamil's wedding. Apart from its elaborate detail and its unabashed pinkness, Kimberly and Jamil's save-the-date clearly implied the importance of their faith and their wedding as a religious ceremony.

We worked with Two Blue Doors in St Louis for this one. The shape was an oversized rectangular matchbook that slid shut at the top. The cover was engraved with 1 Corinthians 13:7-8. The top was woven with hot-pink double-faced satin ribbon. Inscribed in florid pink script on a lighter pink paper inside were the date and the particulars. The envelopes were a heavy white stock lined with the same pink pattern from the interior of the save-the-date. All calligraphy was done in hot pink.

Such a stylized save-the-date set the bar for what was to follow with the wedding invitation. Kim wanted to be sure it was something no one in St. Louis had ever seen before. For the invitation and the remaining papery we collaborated with my immensely talented friend Karen Bartolomei from Grapevine to create something fabulous. Kim loved the idea of incorporating her initials into the design. We came up with the idea of having a square invitation "pocket" open on a diagonal with the bride's initials on a die-cut circle that slid together at the center. The paper for the outer "pocket" was letterpress printed in two colors of custom-mixed pink, in a decorative, Florentine-inspired grapevine pattern. The invitation inside was a heavy cream-colored card engraved in pink and metallic gold, on the diagonal, with the same Florentine-inspired grapevine motif. For those of you who know anything about printing—we had Karen on the run. In retrospect, I can't think of a printing technique we *didn't* use in the creation of Kimberly's papery collection. We specially printed patterned paper to make the outer mailing envelopes, which were lined by hand with imported metallic gold paper. We used Xandra Y. Zamora of XYZ Ink in Southern California. The ink was custom-mixed, and Xandra scripted it with an unerringly agile hand.

# The Papery

## THE PAPERY FOR A WEDDING IS THE FIRST AND LAST FORMAL COMMUNICATION

*your guests receive from you; the first being your save-the-date card or invitation, the last being your thank-you note for their wedding gift. As I have said before I think of the papery as a suite, unified by one or more of your wedding's design Elements. The interesting thing, conversely, is that as the thread that ties the wedding events together, the papery also unifies the wedding design. Aside perhaps from the flowers, the papery is one of the most important components in which your effort and attention to detail is tangible and appreciated. It bears the imprint of your creative signature, your personal style, and your hospitality, and it is something every guest touches and on some level interacts with. As you have seen throughout the pages of this book, I strongly believe your papery is worth all the time and investment you can give it, because unlike other components of your wedding—the food, the music, even the flowers—the papery is permanent. Every single piece is a keepsake, created for and by you as a symbol of one of the most special days of your life.*

MR. AND MRS. DAVID LLOYD STEWARD
REQUEST THE HONOUR OF YOUR PRESENCE
AT THE MARRIAGE CEREMONY OF THEIR DAUGHTER

*Kimberly Elizabeth*
*to*
*Jamil Steven Blackwell*

SATURDAY, THE EIGHTEENTH OF FEBRUARY
TWO THOUSAND AND SIX
AT FOUR O'CLOCK IN THE AFTERNOON
SALEM UNITED METHODIST CHURCH IN LADUE
SAINT LOUIS, MISSOURI

*Recept*

DIN
IMMEDIATE!

BLACK

*W*ouldn't you know the wedding day went on record as the coldest day in St. Louis in twenty years? And New York was pelted with a heavy snowfall the day before we were to leave . . . *oy!* The elaborate fresh flowers we had designed for outside both the church and country club had to be rethought at the last minute as most fresh flowers will not withstand extreme temperatures. We managed just fine and no one was the wiser. The floral wreaths that were to hang on the church doors were moved to the balcony where the gospel choir was seated, fitting in beautifully just beneath a floral garland.

Once inside the church the grim chill of the winter night warmed to the glow of candlelight and the brightness of spring blossoms. Lining the central aisle were six-foot-tall standards alternately swathed in deep and light shades of pink chiffon. With hot-pink wire we attached pink cymbidiums to the fabric in a descending spiral, landing softly at the bottom in a soft chiffon pool. At the top were globe arrangements of pink James Story orchids, Majolica roses, Lovely Lydia spray roses, white anemones, pink lisianthus, and silvery pink roses.

# *Grace Notes*

## THE MOST PHOTOGENIC, THE MOST EXTRAVAGANT, THE MOST EXPENSIVE,

*the most lavishly designed wedding in the world will only be truly beautiful if it is truly joyful, and that joy emanates from you and your family. Do not get so caught up in your wedding planning that you lose sight of the big picture. On the morning of her wedding Kimberly's father cooked a special breakfast just for the two of them at home so that they could have some one-on-one time together before all the hoopla. Of all*

*Kimberly's wedding memories, I will bet that this stands out as one of her fondest.*

*Take time with your fiancé, your family, and your friends to let them know how much you love and appreciate them. These are the grace notes of life and the sweetest music there is.*

At the pews were bunches of bush ivy, Lovely Lydia roses, and James Story orchids gathered together with hot-pink double-faced satin ribbon. Bush ivy, which in winter is laden with dark blue berries, is a highly satisfactory green to use this time of year as it offers excellent texture and depth. We employed it throughout the church and club to great effect.

At the altar rail we introduced our Element of grapevine, weaving and spiraling it among clusters of bush ivy and bunches of pink Majolica and Lovely Lydia roses. The altar itself was flanked by a pair of four-foot-tall pedestals supporting large white iron urns arranged with pink quince, hot-pink hydrangea, and pink French tulips. The guests had much to take in and the ceremony had not even begun!

The wedding program was a tall rectangle bound at the top with heavy gold satin ribbon. The cream-colored paper cover was letterpress printed with our vine pattern and engraved in two shades of pink. The inside cover liner was in hot-pink vellum and the cream pages were offset printed in gold metallic ink.

The groomsmen wore boutonnieres of winter berries, pink quince, and twigs, wound with hot-pink ribbon and fastened with gold wire.

The maids of honor carried Hot Lady roses (which I somehow could not bring myself to tell the bride), fuchsia ranunculus, pink James Story orchids, and Lovely Lydia spray roses. Light pink satin ribbon with a hot-pink French twist finished the bouquet.

With the ceremony behind them, the bridal couple was driven to the reception in style, complete with a pretty, hand-painted JUST MARRIED sign.

For the flower girls we made the most divine hanging globes consisting of pink Majolica roses and pink hyacinths studded with white pearl centers. We made handles and streamers of pink double-faced satin ribbon, the latter threaded with gold wire and individual pink hyacinth blossoms. The stunning little floral spheres perfectly matched the girls' two-tone pink dresses, and they seemed terribly pleased with their adorable selves.

195

The bridal bouquet was a compact arrangement of white stephanotis with pink crystal centers, pink and white sweet pea, Titanic roses, and gardenias wound with pale pink double-faced satin ribbon. As Kimberly prepared to walk down the aisle, a seventy-five-foot pink dupioni silk runner monogrammed with the couple's initials was unfurled to signal her procession.

The ceremony was as important to Kimberly and Jamil as it was to their respective families, and as you see we put a tremendous amount of time into giving it the design emphasis they desired. Aside from the visual elements—the dresses, flowers, and papery—music was an integral part of the evening. A gospel choir sang hymns especially chosen by Kimberly's mother, Thelma, to accompany the seating of the grandparents and parents. The bride processed to Clarke's "Trumpet Voluntaire" accompanied by solo trumpeter Robert Souza and organist Mary Hitchcock-Reinhart. When the vows were said and the blessing given, the newly married couple recessed to the choir's rousing rendition of "O Happy Day." And to the chagrin of the ladies present who happened to wear mascara, there wasn't a dry eye in the house.

Kimberly and Jamil also chose to honor the old African-American tradition of jumping the broom, which signifies that all past problems have been swept away. We, of course, put our imprint on the broom and wrapped the handle with pink ribbons. And then we all were smitten with the broom bearer, Camden, who at first couldn't understand why the bride was "jumping the groom!"

# Music

IF YOU ARE A MOVIE LOVER AS I AM, YOU UNDERSTAND WELL HOW IMPORTANT

the music can be to the overall emotional and artistic statement of the film. It is not by accident that every movie has a soundtrack and that some of those soundtracks become stand-alone creative statements themselves. So strong is the power of music in telling a story that I encourage you not to underestimate it in telling yours. Music as an afterthought sounds like an afterthought (if it is listened to at all), but music deliberately and carefully thought out is one of the greatest gifts you can give yourself as well as your guests.

We have touched upon music in other chapters, noting where local custom or family tradition might strike a certain musical note to help set the tone and mood of the weekend. For our Bahamas wedding the bride booked the local Junkanoo band to lead the wedding party from the ceremony to the reception. And for our couple married in Vermont a fiddle player called the tune.

For our St. Louis wedding the music was a key component. From salsa to gospel, to Motown, to hip-hop, this wedding had it covered and the crowd was thrilled by it. Inspired by the music and moved by its rhythm, the guests seemed all the more caught up in the joy and the spirit of each event.

To begin the rehearsal dinner, the bride's parents and her fiancé surprised everyone with a salsa band—the bride's favorite—ay caramba! The gospel choir singing during the ceremony was as moving as anything I have ever witnessed in a wedding. I will never forget "O Happy Day" at the end. During the reception, the soft and sultry voice of a jazz vocalist entertained, but not so loudly that people could not talk. After dinner, the band struck up and guests danced their hearts out to Motown classics and crowd-pleasing oldies. As the night progressed, so did the style of music, and by late night a DJ was spinning hip-hop tunes. Decorum was restored by evening's end when the horn player from the church returned to give the newlyweds a tuneful sendoff.

Regardless of your musical inclinations, do give this aspect of your festivities considerable thought sooner rather than later. Work with the musical director at your church or synagogue to determine the music you want for your ceremony. Do you want a choir or a soloist? Might your Uncle Andrew play the bagpipes? Do you need to track down your old college roommate to find out what she had for her processional that you liked so much? And for the reception, if there is a particular band or DJ you want, book them as far in advance as you can. Local and regional booking agencies have scores of possibilities for musical entertainment appropriate for a range of budgets—inquire of country club managers and others who are responsible for booking bands at parties and other events. And if you have a DJ, begin keeping a list of your and your fiancé's favorite songs so the DJ can be prepared to accommodate your requests.

One last thing: People have come to your wedding to celebrate you and to socialize. Don't make it difficult for them by making it impossible for them to talk—or more to the point, to hear. Older guests find too-loud music impossible to tolerate and others find it simply irritating and inconsiderate. Keep the volume to a reasonable level.

As I mentioned, the cold kept us from going ahead with our flower plans for the outside of the country club, so in order to create that "wow" effect everybody was going for, I ended up renting a generator at the last minute and flooding the front of the country club with pink light. When you approached it from the start of the long driveway it was a real stunner.

Fortunately the club entry had a wonderful double staircase we were able to decorate with swirling grapevine, pink cymbidiums, bush ivy, pink Majolica, Hot Lady, and Lovely Lydia roses. And to really make it pop we lit the entire staircase with pink light. This also created the perfect backdrop for the couple's farewell, with trumpet player, Rolls-Royce, and all!

Once the guests rounded the staircase corner they came upon the seating card table, which, as I have stated repeatedly, should have maximum visual impact. Ours here was an eight-foot-long table covered in hot-pink silk linen and holding three arrangements in sixteen-inch square metallic gold vases filled with silvery pink roses, pink cymbidiums, pink sweet pea, pink roses, and bush ivy. The arrangements were connected by lengths of grapevine and wired with pink cymbidiums.

Reprising the diagonal design element from the invitation, we thought exaggerating that shape for the seating cards would be exciting and fresh—and it was—especially with more than three hundred cards all lined up together. Paper-meister Karen carried the vine pattern and pink paper from the invite to the pocket of the seating card. Guests' names were written in hot-pink calligraphy on a cream card.

199

*K*imberly made us swear not to let a soul into the dining room before they were officially invited in for dinner. She wanted to be the first to see the room! A sea of hot-pink dupioni-draped tables were surrounded by gold ballroom chairs and lit by clusters of three-, six-, and nine-inch gold pillar candles and frosted pink votives. At each place setting a gold charger held a hot-pink-and-gold napkin enfolding the dinner menu. A single pink cymbidium was placed alongside.

*W*e created three different centerpieces, continuing with the flowers and greenery used in the church and the bridal flowers, adding to them with viburnum, hot-pink stock, and snapdragons.

The first and most striking centerpiece was mounted on a three-foot hourglass-shaped vase with a grapevine and cymbidium spiral inside. At the base of the tall centerpiece were six smaller satellite arrangements in pink pearlized vases of roses wired with pink crystals. The second centerpiece was a two-foot glass vase with a grapevine and orchid scroll inside, encircled at the base by a grapevine wreath and clusters of hot-pink roses and bush ivy. The final design was a low arrangement in a glass compote, again with a grapevine wreath at its base and clusters of roses and ivy.

*K*im really loved her monogram and wanted to carry it throughout her wedding design details, including the dinner menu. We letterpressed the cover in pink with her metallic gold monogram in a circle and then the interior menu on cream stock with metallic gold engraving and heading engraved in fuschia ink.

*T*his brings us to food. I love nothing more than to see a family with the confidence and spirit to create a menu that reflects something about their family history or the couple's ethnicity. Kimberly's family's culinary roots were in good old-fashioned Southern cooking. We spent months research-ing the dinner menu and what to have for hors d'oeuvres. We needed to find the perfect marriage between the past and the present.

The Wedding Feast

LOUISIANA CAJUN
DUCK GUMBO

TOSSED BABY GREENS
Marinated Cucumbers and Tomatoes
Honey Mustard Vinaigrette

TRADITIONAL SOUTHERN
FRIED CHICKEN
Whipped Sweet Potatoes
Braised Collard Greens
Whipped Potatoes
Southern Pan Gravy

Cornbread Muffins, Caramel Rolls
Focaccia and Buttermilk Biscuits

WINE SELECTION
N.V. Billecart Salmon Rose, France
2004 Solitude Chardonnay, Carneros
2004 Wishing Tree Shiraz, Australia

WEDDING CAKE
Coffee and Tea

FEBRUARY 18, 2006

*D*inner was fried chicken, sweet potatoes, braised collard greens, mashed potatoes, and pan-fried gravy. And I can tell you there wasn't a plate that didn't go back to the kitchen clean. Kimberly's mom also had us order bottles of Vidalia Onion and Peach Hot Sauce from a Georgia company called Prissy's of Vidalia for the tables. It was a delicious complement to the main course.

*O*nce guests were called into dinner, we replaced the seating card table with an old glass and wood bakery case we brought from New York. From the start Kim wanted to create a personalized sweet treat for her guests as they left the reception. Along with her grandmother's favorite recipes, she sent me Web site sources for pink bakery boxes—which were ordered and assembled, thanks in great part to our trusty baker, Pat. Then it was up to Karen and me to create a concept that would capture the entire evening in one small package. We ended up custom-printing our vine pattern on hot-pink vellum that was cut to the size of the bakery boxes. To finish them off we made a crack-and-peel sticker with the vine pattern design and the newlyweds' names in the center. And when you opened up the box, there were not only cookies and treats but accordion-folded recipes printed on cream paper in hot-pink ink, of course, all for a sweet, pink finish.

*I* often leave the cake design for the latter part of the design process as it encompasses so many of the wedding details. Pat Rutherford-Pettine from Sugaree Baking Company right in St. Louis is one of our favorite bakers. A character and a real talent, Pat must have endured fifteen or more cake design suggestions before we finally settled on the obvious and used the paper pattern from the invitation. The cake was an elegant tower of buttercream and fondant. Feminine and sophisticated at the same time—just right.

*K*imberly and Jamil's sweetheart table was placed atop an eight-foot-long platform covered in hot-pink fabric. We had the lighting company create a gobo (like a monogrammed spotlight) of the couple's initials that projected onto the center of the dance floor.

*I* did a little poking around about the meaning of the color pink. Pink is the color of universal love, representing friendship and affection. Pink is gentle, casual, and approachable. It is no surprise to me that pink is Kimberly's favorite color, and I can say with certainty that the guests at this go-all-out wedding left feeling wholeheartedly "in the pink."

# High Seas and
## Vintage Romance

ow does a Coast Guard lieutenant on active duty who spends his nights in graduate school meet a tech company marketing director who spends her nights at dance class and her free time training for triathlons? On the Internet, of course. Though neither Dan Somma nor Soley Hartel really expected to meet their future spouses in cyberspace, Danny saw Soley's photo and was taken by her smile. Since her profile hinted at common interests, Danny initiated e-conversation and eventually the two agreed to get together. Self-professed bookworms both, the pair predictably met at a Barnes & Noble, and after twenty minutes or so of milling about they decided to have dinner. Soley took him to her favorite little Italian spot and the couple were the last to leave. As Soley walked with Danny to the subway, he asked if she was free for Saturday and then leaned down and kissed her . . . whereupon she darted off into the night, sprinting across six lanes of traffic—not exactly the response he was hoping for. He claims she says she wanted to make the light; she later confesses she was overcome.

The second date sealed their fate as the evening seeped into the wee hours over cinnamon-scented coffee outside the Moondance Diner. When Danny brought Soley home, he asked her to brunch the following day (well, it already was the following day), and she said not until after noon. He rang at 12:02. After eating, the couple walked to the park and talked for hours and hours. Then Soley went back to her apartment and told her roommate she would marry Danny.

For most couples I work with the process of discovering the design Elements is a lengthy one. It can also be somewhat taxing because I am asking them to think in ways they may not have thought before. But with Soley and Danny their thinking was so aligned that the Elements came easily and quickly. Avid travelers and seafarers, their mutual love for all things maritime combined nicely with their bent toward history and penchant for storytelling. Vintage pieces and old nautical charts and maps seemed to be heading the couple in a promising design direction.

## Season:

Winter

## Setting:

State University of New York Maritime College Chapel for ceremony and the New Leaf Café in Fort Tryon Park, New York City, for reception.

## Situation:

A small and intimate late-afternoon wedding with gentlemen in suits and officers in dress whites, followed by a reception and buffet dinner for eighty at a favorite local restaurant.

## Ideas and Inspirations

| | | | | | | | |
|---|---|---|---|---|---|---|---|
| NAUTICAL | COFFEE | CINNAMON | CHOCOLATE | VINTAGE | POSTCARDS | BROOCHES | TRAVEL |
| OLD WORLD | WEATHERED TRUNKS | STEAMER TRUNKS | LUGGAGE | TAGS | DESTINATION LABELS | PARK | SIMPLE |
| WHITE | STONE | MARITIME | NAUTICAL CHARTS | CELESTIAL NAVIGATION | LIGHT-HOUSES | LANTERNS | HISTORY |

# The Elements

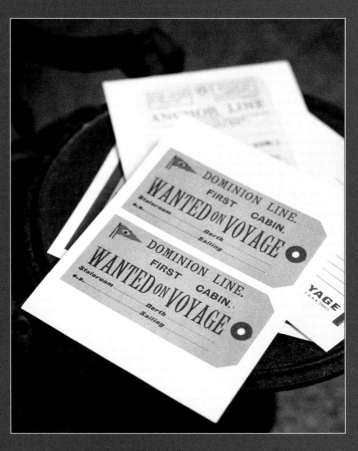

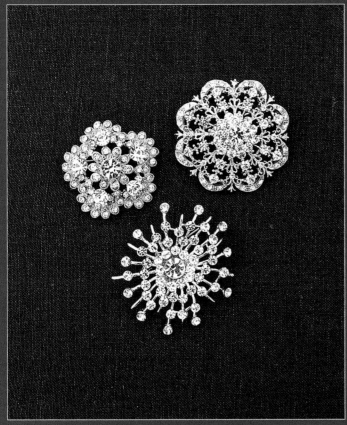

# The Elements

### SHIPS' LANTERNS

Our proud Coast Guard lieutenant commander has picked the right career; he is fascinated with all things maritime, especially the old sailing ships and ocean liners that used to ferry freight and people all around the world. The ship's lantern seemed a fitting emblem to represent the nautical inclinations.

### VINTAGE LUGGAGE TAGS & STICKERS

Both Soley and Danny have been lured in by the romance of the high seas and by the bygone era of elegant travel. Soley began collecting vintage luggage with all the original stickers and tags a few years ago when she inherited a piece from a friend's great-aunt. She even stores her out-of-season clothes in old steamer trunks. Vintage luggage as an Element opens all sorts of accessory possibilities, a favorite and versatile one of which is the vintage luggage tag.

### VINTAGE JEWELRY

Following ocean liners and elegant travel, a fondness for sartorial finery must be close behind. Soley also loves the old shipping line posters picturing stylishly dressed men and women promenading the deck of a luxury cruise ship, lounging in a deck chair, or perhaps passing by the Sphinx on camelback. Vintage jewelry as an Element is a way to capture the flavor of this nostalgic chic, and I find that beautiful old brooches have a number of interesting uses.

### MAPS

As it turns out, and not surprisingly, Danny collects all sorts of old maps and charts. The antique ones often have exquisite insignia and illustrations and make for handsome backgrounds or coverings. As a lifelong sailor myself, I embraced the notion of charts and maps as a design Element.

# The Colors

COPPERY BRONZE

SCARLET

NAVY BLUE

IVORY

# The Details

When it came to the wedding invitation, Soley and Danny decided to create their own design. It was one of several gifts they would present their guests, as they felt it was an expression of their gratitude to friends and family for sharing their affection and the honor of their presence. It was Danny's idea to use stem cuttings from roses he had given to his betrothed as the binding at the top. The couple assembled the pieces themselves and Danny hand addressed them all. He set up a little station in the apartment and spent his free time with his ruler, mechanical pencils, eraser, and ink pen. They received many compliments on the addressing alone.

Danny earned his master's in transportation management from State University of New York Maritime College in 2005. Following his graduation ceremony he and Soley ambled idly over to the SUNY chapel to take a look. The tiny chapel was empty as they approached the altar hand-in-hand. They turned to look at each other and knew this was the place they would eventually exchange their vows.

oley's bouquet was stunning. She wanted to bring an amber-orange into the mix, which at first I feared would be too stark a contrast. But as it often organically happens, that beautiful warm color found its way throughout the wedding design. The bouquet was composed of sweet pea, white Majolica roses, ranunculus, and orange calla lilies. My design director, Kim, handpicked three bejeweled brooches to fasten to the stems with ivory double-faced satin ribbon crisscrossed with coppery-orange ribbon.

he flower girls carried small pails dressed up in blue and white ribbon, white yarn, and white river pebbles. (There go our stones again.) Filling the buckets were blue hydrangea sepals—the color of the sea.

The boutonnieres were white sweet pea wrapped with a multitoned grosgrain ribbon. We affixed tiny anchors with a blue pearl pin, which I couldn't resist photographing propped with my beloved grandfather's old block and tackle in the background.

With fifteen-foot arched brick ceilings and light streaming through stained glass windows depicting classic maritime motifs, this small, sturdy chapel was an ideal choice for the couple's intimate ceremony. Otherwise serving as a nonsectarian meditation room for the SUNY student body, the chapel was converted in 1959 from an old casemate in the outer works of Fort Schuyler.

It is interesting to note that both the chapel where Soley and Dan were married and the restaurant where they held their reception are made of stone. The bride especially liked stone and it became almost a fifth Element as it appears in various guises in their wedding design.

In military weddings it is customary for the gentlemen in uniform to raise a sword arch through which the couple passes as they exit the church, but because it was so cold outside, the arch was reinstated at the reception. Like many United States military traditions, the sword arch is adopted from the British, and each branch of the military has its version. The raised and crossed swords symbolize the officers' pledge of loyalty to the newly married couple. As the swords of the arch literally cover and protect the pair, the guard will cover and protect its own. Coast Guard tradition decrees that as the bride and groom pass through the arch, the last two bearers drop their swords, forming a cross to block the couple's path. The groom then kisses his bride, and the swords are raised to permit the couple to walk ahead. As bride and groom proceed, the bearer on the bride's side gently swats her backside and says, "Welcome to the Coast Guard, ma'am."

# "A-tennn-tion!"

*Normally a gentleman escorts a lady on his right, but a gentleman in uniform escorts her on his left, leaving his right hand free to render and return salutes.*

The forecast all day had been for a blizzard, but Mother Nature was merciful and the snow held off until the guests had safely arrived at the reception. (Going home was another matter, however!) Steps away from sweeping views of the Hudson River, in the heart of Fort Tryon Park, the New Leaf Café is in a historic, storybook-looking stone and slate-roofed structure designed by the Olmsted Brothers firm in the 1930s. While it has a distinctly Old World feel and is in a secluded rustic setting, the café and park are still in Manhattan and a longtime favorite of the bride's.

We filled the rooms with candlelight in the form of votives, pillar candles, and ships' lanterns.

Our centerpieces were arranged in clear glass vases—for this sea-loving couple we wanted the water to show! Against the soft blue linen of the tablecloth, the deep periwinkle blue hydrangea, white stock, and white cymbidiums were set off nicely. We added river stones again, because the bride loves all things stone and they looked beautiful and just unusual enough to make a quiet style statement. We also propped a snippet of blue hydrangea at each place setting.

The cocktail table arrangements were navy-blue glass bowls, each floating a gardenia, such a sweet, classic vintage flower. Surrounding each gardenia were votive candles wrapped with small sections of antique maps.

A small vintage travel case we scored on eBay was the ideal conduit to house the collection of vintage luggage tag and travel sticker Elements for guests to write well wishes on to the newlywed couple. The case itself came lined in a colorful map paper and the outside covered in travel stickers—perfect! We supplied the fountain pen and inkwell and the bride supplied the squeal of delight. This is definitely Soley's kind of keepsake!

# Guest Books

**THE GUEST BOOK IS CONSIDERED BY SOME A RELIC OF VICTORIAN TIMES,** *a quaint social custom soon to become dust gatherer that serves no practical purpose. But many a bride would like some way to remember all the people who showed up for her special day. In my constant quest to think out of the proverbial box (and guest book), I strive to create a keepsake that will be both meaningful and reflective of the couple's style.*

*We have covered a box in silk and decorated it with hand-painted sea horses to make it decorative enough to display on a shelf and accessible when the notion strikes to stroll again down memory lane. We have had custom puzzles made for guests to write notes on individual pieces. The couple assembles the puzzle and has it framed for posterity. And one of my favorites is to distribute a collection of small, blank-paged books throughout the room where the reception is held—on cocktail tables and lounge furniture, on bars and restroom vanities—anywhere a guest might alight, have a sip of champagne, and pen a note to the wedding couple. When the booklets are collected, preferably in some wonderful box or container, they can be opened and read again and again.*

In lieu of a formal seated dinner, the meal was served buffet-style, allowing guests to mingle and to have a bite when they chose. Vintage bistro-style menu cards were posted around the café, tipping off diners to what they could look forward to.

The guests' favors weren't so much about theme as they were about the couple's passion . . . for coffee, that is. But admittedly coffee also brought them together that night at the Moondance Diner where they sipped java and talked until two. They gave little burlap sacks of coffee beans as gifts at their engagement party, so it only seemed fitting to give the wedding guests a proper coffee scoop. Danny says he has a special place in his heart for the country of Colombia because it is home to his three favorite things—coffee, chocolate, and, by ancestry, Soley.

As the snow danced and swirled outside, hot toddies were served inside, with a selection of white desserts to play off the seamen's white uniforms and, unintentionally, the winter weather.

*S*oley had a hip, vintage style and her gift choices derived from that style reflected the period we strove to create for her wedding. Soley even told her fiancé she wanted a ring "like you might find in Grandma's attic."

For their wedding party, Soley and Danny chose vintage cufflinks for the best man and beautiful compact mirrors and vintage perfume bottles for the ladies. Their choices demonstrated thought and care but didn't break the bank.

She also gave her bridesmaids cashmere shawls with vintage brooches to fasten them and chicly stave off the chill.

To introduce Soley's gift to Danny, a little history is in order. The couple had gone to Nantucket for a holiday the previous summer to visit family and to . . . Danny had his scheme all set but Soley thought they were just going for a walk on the beach. When she sensed something was up, Danny dropped down to one knee. "Soley, will you marry me—please, please, please?"

When it came to Danny's gift the source was obvious to me: master illustrator and calligrapher Pier Gustafson, based in Boston. I admire all of Pier's work but I am particularly keen on his maps. What could be more heartfelt than a hand-drawn map of Soley and Danny's courtship? In his inimitable fashion, Pier created a work of art composing all the bits and pieces of information we could think of to give him. The map itself is a scroll indicating how, when, and where Danny proposed. There is a drawing of Nantucket on which "X" marks the treasured spot. The compass rose in the upper-right-hand corner bears the couple's initials intertwined, and the border has two stripes and four shields to designate his rank in the Coast Guard. It doesn't get more personal or relevant than that.

# Bridal Party Gifts

## BRIDAL PARTY GIFTS AND GUEST FAVORS SHOULD BE A THOUGHTFUL GESTURE.

*And the more personal they are, the more meaning they have. Does anyone really need another picture frame?*

*Bridal party gifts are one of those cases where more is not necessarily better. Heartfelt and hand-hewn is so effective. That's not to say this isn't a time commitment. We have had family artists create small watercolor paintings on birch collected from the island where the family spends summers. Guests went absolutely crazy for the paintings.*

*We just finished a wedding where we designed boxes of baked goods that included the recipes of both sets of grandmothers. But this just wasn't just any old bakery box.*

*We had the tissue, actually vellum, printed with the pattern from the wedding invitation and cut so it fit just so. We also had custom crack-and-peel labels printed for the box tops and accordion-folded recipes cards inserted. They were adorable and guests were grabbing them two and three at a clip.*

*Also, never underestimate the embroidered canvas bag filled with goodies. People love customized bags as practical keepsakes. But take heed, I have never been able to pull off the stuff that fills the bag for less than fifty to one hundred fifty dollars per bag, and bags themselves are quite expensive.*

The most poignant weddings touch the hearts of those in attendance and make even the most distant relative or friend of a friend feel as if they've known you all their lives. The wedding doesn't have to be small and exclusive to be intimate and personal. The smallest detail and a creative bit of thinking will make an otherwise cookie-cutter wedding into a distinctive, personal affair that reflects who you are and what is important to you as a couple. Your day done your way will make a lasting impression on all.

# Acknowledgments

ROBERT ALLEN—For being the most amazing literary agent on the planet Earth and helping me realize a dream.

KATHLEEN SPINELLI—For always speaking from your heart.

LAUREN MARINO—For seeing the vision from the word go and never wavering. I can't imagine a smarter partner.

HILARY TERRELL—For helping me manage what on many days felt unmanageable.

KIM HIRST—For every minute detail and your complete commitment.

ANTONIA VAN DER MEER—For always being gracious, interested, and completely supportive.

LINDA HIRST—You are so generous of spirit. Thank you for Kim and thank you for absolutely everything (and there is a lot of everything).

LOU DiLORENZO—For teaching me to reach for perfect.

FRANCES SCHULTZ—Thank you for your beautiful word-smithing and our hours of chats about life.

DASHA WRIGHT—Thank you for your amazing eye and patience.

JENNIFER ZABINSKI—For introducing me to Brands to Books. You have been a tremendous support in every facet.

CLAUDIA HANLIN—Thank you for giving me a platform when I really needed it.

KAREN BARTOLOMEI—You are a rock star and über-talented. I know this is the start of many creative projects!

PHIL MANTAS, a.k.a. MacGyver, a.k.a. The Equalizer. Shimmying up the palm tree—impressive!

DARCY MILLER—For always supporting my career no matter what stage.

DOUG TRUPPE—Thank you handling a lot of the icky stuff and keeping it real.

NICOLAS DAEPPEN—Thank you for jumping in at the final hour.

DON CITARELLA—Thanks for being my partner in the original pitch! Didn't change much, did it?

MY MOM—For introducing me to *Sir Gawain and the Green Knight.*

MY DAD—Who has always thought I could do anything.

MY SISTER, PAMELA—For being there whenever I call. And I call.

MY GRANDMOTHER, FAY GERALDINE—For helping me discover my love of entertaining.

BECKY—For endless support and laughter.

RAND—For your friendship, hours of volunteer work, and pep talks.

KEVIN—For always telling me I am ham and cheese on a roll.

DON PURDY & WALLACE TUTT—I just love you both. You are definitely lifetime members of the friends and family club.

JAY JAY PERCENTI—Thank you to the Paris Hilton of Harbour Island! We couldn't have done it without you!

MATTHEW ANDERSON—Aside from always making us feel like the client, thank you for creating complete access for the shoot. You are such a gentleman.

JENNIFER BLUMIN—Thank you for supporting my business at every turn. You are a delight, and damn you for looking so good at the end of a long day.

GINNY CONNELLY—Thank you for introducing me to one of our couples for the book! You know how I love my Jersey shore and I was thrilled to be able to feature a wedding that speaks to my heart.

JEFF FOWLER—Thank you for greasing the wheels and opening up a whole new world!

JOAN BEVER—Thank you for your complete support and leap of faith. You have a big heart.

LYNN BUTLER—Thank you for throwing open the doors and helping us with one heck of a party.

FAUSTO ESPINOSA—For helping me find one of the couples in the book with dress whites, sword arch and all.

RON BEN-ISRAEL—You are definitely my sugar daddy. Creating with you, I daresay . . . takes the cake!

CHERYL KLEINMAN—Thank you for your beautiful, beautiful cake! You are the queen of chic!

LIZ SECURRO—Thank you so much for bringing us one of the couples for the book.

JEFF SERAFINI—To our favorite flower nerd. Your patience and passion for such a tough business makes us look so good!

ANDREW BICKNELL—Thank you for referring me to Miss Maggie. Love that Harbour Island!

JEFFERY WEISSMAN—My dog walker, for taking care of Miss Lola on many long days!

To our amazing freelance design staff:
Deborah Bloom, Evelyn Yepez, Sonia Beltran, Aure Morales and your amazing team, Jenevive Peralta, Jose Zavala, Paco Rodriguez, Suzanne Jacobson, Marjeth Cummings, Billy Hirst, Yoko Kato, Yuko Kawaji, Alana Guglielmo, and Raymundo Maltos. Your creativity and energy made this book possible.

And finally, thank you to ALL OUR BRIDES & GROOMS for sharing your wedding days and all of your creativity. Just beautiful!

Gerri & Brett Lawrence, Steve & Maggie Kennedy, Kimberly & Jamil Blackwell, Heather & Jared Tomlinson, Heather & Matthew Schimenti, Adele & Brendan Cassidy, Jennie & Daniel Jamieson, Taryn & Eduardo Rioseco, Soley & Dan Somma.

223

# Resources

## PAPERY

**Karen Bartolomei for Grapevine**
105 N Street
Boston, Massachusetts 02127
www.grapevineweddings.com
800-994-3799

**Ceci New York**
22 West 23rd Street
Fifth Floor Penthouse
New York, New York 10010
www.cecinewyork.com
212-989-0695

**Peculiar Pair Press**
www.peculiarpairpress.com
415-812-7247
415-407-7247

## CATERERS

**Tentation Potel & Chabot Catering**
524 West 34th Street
New York, New York 10001
www.tentation.net
212-564-7530

**Crane & Co., Inc.**
30 South Street
Dalton, Massachusetts 01226
www.crane.com
800-268-2281

**Dreamland Designs**
1721 Franklin Avenue, SE
Minneapolis, Minnesota 55414
www.dreamland-designs.com
612-341-2586

**Two Blue Doors**
7 Gray Avenue
Webster Groves, Missouri 63119
www.twobluedoors.com
314-968-4033

## CAKES

**Ron Ben-Israel Cakes**
42 Greene Street, 5th Floor
New York, New York 10013
www.weddingcakes.com
212-625-3369

**Cheryl Kleinman Cakes**
448 Atlantic Avenue
Brooklyn, New York 11217
718-237-2271

**Sugaree Baking Company**
1242 Tamm Avenue
St. Louis, Missouri 63139
www.sugareebaking.com
314-645-5496

## WEDDING PLANNERS

**The Wedding Library by Claudia Hanlin & Jennifer Zabinski**
43 East 78th Street
New York, New York 10021
www.theweddinglibrary.com
212-327-0100

**dolce parties**
164 Mason Street
Penthouse
Greenwich, Connecticut 06830
www.dolceparties.com
203-622-3114

## SWEETS & CANDIES

**Mrs. Prindable's Handmade Confections**
Affy Tapple LLC
6300 Gross Point Road
Niles, Illinois  60714
www.mrsprindables.com
866-678-9797

**Magnolia Bakery**
401 Bleecker Street
New York, New York 10014
212-462-2572

**Len Libby Candies**
419 U.S. Route 1
Scarborough, Maine 04074
www.lenlibby.com
207-883-4897

## WEDDING VENUES

**New York Botanical Garden**
Bronx River Parkway at Fordham Road
Bronx, New York 10458
www.nybg.org
718-817-8700

**The Equinox**
3567 Main Street, Route 7A
Manchester Village, Vermont 05254
equinox.rockresorts.com
866-346-ROCK

**Sky Studios**
704 Broadway, Penthouse B
New York, New York 10003
www.skystudios.com
212-533-3030

**Rock House**
Corner of Bay and Hill Street
Harbour Island, Bahamas
www.rockhousebahamas.com
242-333-2053

**The St. Regis Hotel**
2 East 55th Street
New York, New York 10022
www.stregis.com
212-753-4500

**Bonnet Island Estate**
2400 East Bay Avenue
Bonnet Island, New Jersey 08050
www.bonnetislandestate.com
609-494-9100

**DELAMAR Greenwich Harbor**
500 Steamboat Road
Greenwich, Connecticut 06830
www.thedelamar.com
866-335-2627

**The Breakers**
One South County Road
Palm Beach, Florida 33480
www.thebreakers.com
888-BREAKERS

**New Leaf Café**
One Margaret Corbin Drive,
Fort Tryon Park
New York, New York 10040
www.nnyrp.org/newleaf
212-568-5323

## GIFTS

**Marc Blackwell New York**
157 West 26th Street
New York, New York 10001
www.marcblackwell.com
212-696-2827

**BedHead Pajamas**
3305 Motor Avenue
Los Angeles, CA 90034
www.bedheadpjs.com
310-280-1080

**Prissy's of Vidalia**
P.O. Box 1213
Vidalia, Georgia   30475
www.prissys.com
800-673-7372

## LINENS

**Magnolias Linens**
316 East 84th Street
New York, New York 10028
www.magnoliasgroup.com
212-472-7708

**Triserve Party Rentals**
www.triservepartyrentals.com
718-822-1930